Golden Retrievers

Edie MacKenzie

BARRON'S

Acknowledgments

The writing of this book was greatly facilitated by the kindness and wisdom of many people. Rhonda Hovan, of Faera Golden Retrievers and the GRCA, generously lent her valuable expertise in the realms of breeding and Golden Retriever health. Anna Geisler of Bone Adventure was a great help making connections. The information about rescues and rescue placement from Jane Nygaard, Cynthia Erickson, and Louise Dobbe of RAGOM was invaluable. And lastly, the hunting education I received from Wolf Smith of Wolf River Griffons and Just Paws Puppy Training, Beryl Board of RAGOM, Tom Brunes of Pet Stuff, Dwight Miller, and Derek Prchal was eye opening and fascinating. My deepest gratitude to them all.

About the Author

Edie MacKenzie lives in Minnesota with her husband, three dogs, and nine tortoises. She has written six e-books, numerous articles, and her first book with Barron's, *Goldendoodles: A Complete Pet Owner's Manual*, since becoming a full-time writer in 2005. Her fascination is the critical correlation between good breeding and canine health. She has a soft spot in her heart for old dogs and rescues.

Dedication

To Jane Nygaard, who, more than 25 years ago, founded Retrieve a Golden of Minnesota (RAGOM), and to all the dedicated RAGOM volunteers, who have helped countless Goldens find their forever homes. So many happy tails, waving their beautiful golden plumes!

All information and advice contained in this book has been reviewed by a veterinarian.

A Word About Pronouns

Many dog lovers feel that the pronoun "it" is not appropriate when referring to a pet that can be such a wonderful part of our lives. For this reason the Golden Retriever in this book is referred to as "Sadie" and "she" unless the topic specifically relates to male dogs. This by no means infers any preference, nor should it be taken as an indication that either sex is particularly problematic.

Cover Credits

Tara Darling: back cover; Shutterstock: front cover.

Photo Credits

Beryl Board: page 167; Seth Casteel: pages 15, 21, 35, 43, 63, 65, 110, 146, 171; Kent Dannen: pages 17, 30, 78, 84, 102, 134, 149; Jean Fogle: pages 3, 33, 89, 97, 114, 137, 143, 145, 173; Daniel Johnson/Paulette Johnson: pages 126 (top, bottom), 127 (top, bottom), 128 (top, bottom), 129 (top, bottom), 130 (top, bottom), 131 (top, bottom), 165; Paulette Johnson: pages 50, 99; Pets by Paulette: page 5; Shutterstock: pages i, iii, vi, 6, 7, 8, 12, 20, 23, 24, 26, 29, 36, 38, 41, 56, 61, 93, 105, 108, 113, 117, 121, 124, 132, 151, 158, 161, 168, 174, 178; SmartPakCanine.com: pages 152, 156, 164; Connie Summers: pages 66, 70, 138; Angela Tartaro: pages 45, 46, 53, 55, 58, 162.

Photos on pages 2 and 4 are courtesy of the Anne and Herbert A. Willis archives.

Kennel Club—Retriever (Golden) Breed Standard on page 10 is reprinted with permission of The Kennel Club.

All inquiries should be addressed to:
Barron's Educational Series, Inc.
250 Wireless Boulevard
Hauppauge, New York 11788
www.barronseduc.com

ISBN-10: 0-7641-4492-8 (Book)
ISBN-13: 978-0-7641-4492-9 (Book)
ISBN-10: 0-7641-8678-7 (DVD)
ISBN-13: 978-0-7641-8678-3 (DVD)
ISBN-10: 0-7641-9771-1 (Package)
ISBN-13: 978-0-7641-9771-0 (Package)

Library of Congress Catalog Card No: 2009053216

Library of Congress Cataloging-in-Publication Data
MacKenzie, Edie.
   Golden retrievers / Edie MacKenzie.
      p. cm. — (Barron's dog bibles)
   Includes index.
   ISBN-13: 978-0-7641-4492-9
   ISBN-10: 0-7641-4492-8
   ISBN-13: 978-0-7641-8678-3
   ISBN-10: 0-7641-8678-7
   1. Golden retriever—Juvenile literature. I. Title.
   SF429.G63M25 2010
   636.752'7—dc22   2009053216

Printed in China

9 8 7 6 5 4 3 2

CONTENTS

CONTENTS

T he Golden Retriever, like all dog breeds, was created to fill a human need. The origin of this breed can be traced to the nineteenth century, when the advancement of gun technology first allowed hunters to successfully shoot birds in flight. This development created the need for a field dog to flush birds into the air, travel a wide range or go into deep water in order to locate them, and then retrieve the birds without causing additional damage to it.

The first Lord Tweedmouth of Scotland is credited with developing the Golden Retriever during the late nineteenth century through careful, selective breeding, and, in the decades following their development, Golden Retrievers remained in the domain of sportsmen. In 1932, they were recognized by the American Kennel Club, and 1938 saw the founding of the Golden Retriever Club of America. It wasn't until the latter part of the twentieth century that Golden Retrievers became popular companion dogs.

In so many ways, the skills and temperament of this amazing hunting dog have successfully translated to the pace and needs of our modern world. The calm, gentle temperament of the Golden Retriever makes her ideally suited for families. Having been bred as a steady field dog, a Golden Retriever has remarkable nerves, which neither the noise and chaos of a hunt nor an active family will rattle. This steadiness also makes Goldens superb service and assistance dogs. Ever amiable, Goldens won't be terrific guard dogs, but as companions and working dogs, they are without peer.

Goldens have a compliant nature and are easy to train, which makes them a good choice for the first-time dog owner. Although Goldens enjoy people and would never turn down the offer of a pat on the head from a stranger, they prefer the praise and encouragement inherent in a close relationship with a kind owner. The Golden's brainpower—they rank in the top five for canine intelligence—can lead to mischief if the dog is not adequately engaged, so owners must be committed to ongoing activities and training.

Without a doubt, it is Golden Retrievers' intuitive nature that earns them a place in our hearts as beloved companions. It is also the reason why they are highly prized as therapy dogs. Their ability to sense a person's mood and act as a cheerleader, a clown, or a shoulder to cry on, depending on the need, is indeed very special.

Popular around the globe, the Golden Retriever has a versatility that few dogs can match. Whether you are thinking about getting a Golden Retriever or already have one, this book will help you care for your Golden and, hopefully, give you a glimpse of her fantastic potential.

Chapter One

All About Golden Retrievers

When Lord Tweedmouth developed the Golden Retriever on his remote estate in Scotland, he never could have envisioned the impact his talented hunting dog would have on the world. Let's look back at the development of the Golden Retriever with a bit of history and a dash of storytelling.

A Little Gundog History

In Victorian England, country hunting estates had become very fashionable among the wealthy. Each estate typically had a kennel master, who was responsible for the health and well-being of the dogs used during the hunts. The preferred dogs for flushing and retrieving birds were heavier-boned versions of today's setters and spaniels. Gun technology at the time required the hunter to be rather close to the bird, and he generally was able to net about a dozen or so birds in a day.

In the late 1800s, the introduction of the break-action shotgun represented a significant advancement over the muzzle loading guns of the day because, for the first time, hunters were able to shoot birds in flight. However, since the downed birds were now further away from the hunter and his dogs, finding birds presented a logistical problem and thus the need for a new type of retrieving dog. This new dog would need to:

- stay quietly with the hunter or range ahead to flush game, depending on whether the birds being hunted were in the weeds or flying overhead;
- have steady nerves to tolerate gunshot at very close range,
- visually mark the descent of the shot bird and locate it;
- have a biddable nature and be able to take direction from her handler while far afield;
- problem solve and think independently in the field;
- have a strong nose to search out the downed bird, whether on land or in the water;

- be a strong swimmer with a water-resistant coat for water retrievals; and
- have a soft mouth so as not to further damage the bird when bringing it back to the hunter.

Oh, and she must also have the stamina to do this all day long, day after day. Phew! What a tall order!

The Golden Retriever Story

It is believed that, over time, other breeds were introduced into the Golden Retriever lines to strengthen various characteristics, including the Irish Setter (bird sense and coat), the Newfoundland (strength and endurance), and the Bloodhound (superior scenting ability).

And now the Golden Retriever's story begins. It isn't often the development of a breed can be fully traced, but this is the case for the Golden Retriever, thanks to the meticulous records of the breed's founder, Sir Dudley Coutts Marjoribanks, the first Lord Tweedmouth. Lord Tweedmouth's studbooks and notes of came to light in the early 1950s, when his descendants made them public, and they are now in possession of the Kennel Club of the United Kingdom.

Lord Tweedmouth was an avid hunter and owned a 20,000-acre hunting estate, called Guisachan, in the Scottish Highlands near Loch Ness. In

1866, he bought a yellow Wavy Coat Retriever (now known as the Flat-coated Retriever) named Nous (Gaelic for "wisdom") from a cobbler in Brighton. (The breed is usually black, but a recessive gene does occasionally produce yellow pups.) In 1868, Lord Tweedmouth bred Nous to Belle, a Tweed Water Spaniel. Now extinct, the breed was very popular with hunters in the region at the time because of its high intelligence, great temperament, water-resistant coat, and tremendous swimming ability. Of the resulting four yellow puppies, Cowslip and Primrose stayed on Lord Tweedmouth's estate for breeding, and thus became the progenitors of the Golden Retriever.

After 21 years of thoughtful breeding, two puppies born in 1889; Prim and Rose, were the last dogs bred by the first Lord Tweedmouth and are

considered the foundational dogs of all future Golden Retrievers. Culham Kennels was founded by Lord Harcourt using Culham Brass and Culham Rossa, both of whom were descendants of Prim and Rose. From there the popularity of the Golden took hold, and several prominent English citizens continued breeding Golden Retrievers. Around the globe, all Golden Retrievers originate from British stock.

As early as 1904, the first Golden Retriever won a field trial. It was also in 1904 that the Kennel Club (Britain's national all-breed club) recognized the Golden Retriever, but only as a variation of the Wavy (Flat) Coat Retriever; in 1913 the Golden was recognized as a unique breed, known as the Golden or Yellow Retriever. In addition, 1913 saw the formation of the Golden Retriever Club of England. The "Yellow" was officially dropped from the name in 1920, and the breed name Golden Retriever was fully established.

Breed Truths

The year 1995 was a wonderful one for Golden Retriever historians and enthusiasts! Lord Harcourt's Culham Kennel pedigrees were discovered among his papers in an Oxford library,confirming the link between his Culham Kennels foundation dogs and Lord Tweedmouth's Rose.

Goldens in North America

Goldens came to the United States in the 1890s, when the Honorable Archie Marjoribanks, Lord Tweedmouth's son, brought a Golden named Lady to his ranch in Texas. Other Goldens came to the United States and Canada during the early 1900s, but none of them were registered with a kennel club.

In 1925, the first Golden Retriever was registered with the American Kennel Club (AKC). However, it wasn't until 1932 that the Golden Retriever was recognized as a separate breed.

Colonel S. S. Magoffin and his wife, both originally from Minnesota, played a significant role in establishing the Golden Retriever in North America through their Rockhaven Kennel in North Vancouver, Canada.

Magoffin owned the first Golden AKC champion, Speedwell Pluto, as well as the second and third champions.

While Goldens slowly gained popularity throughout the United States and Canada, the Midwest— particularly Minnesota—became the epicenter of Golden Retriever growth. Minnesota, a state with huge tracks of farmland and prairie, is also known as the Land of 10,000 Lakes, and it is a hunter's paradise for upland game birds and water-fowl. Add to this, natural migration patterns that follow the Great Lakes and the Mississippi River, and it is no wonder the Midwest hunt-ers embraced the versatile Golden Retriever.

Golden Retriever Club of America (GRCA) The Golden Retriever Club of America (GRCA) was formed in the Midwest in 1938 and has been an advocate for Golden Retriever standards and health ever since. Most notably, the GRCA conducts intensive health studies for the purpose of improving the future health of the breed. (Information on how you can participate in these studies with your Golden Retriever can be found in the Resources section.)

Increasing Popularity

The onset of World War II prompted many European breeders to send their Goldens to the United States to keep them safe. Once the war was over, quite a few of these dogs remained here.

The Golden Retriever saw a steady growth in general popularity after the war, but it remained primarily in the provinces of the show ring and the field. However, that all changed in 1974 when President Gerald Ford's daughter, Susan, brought Liberty, a field line Golden Retriever from Minnesota to the White House. Liberty, and her litter of puppies born in 1975, became the canine darlings of the United States, and the Golden Retriever has been a perennial favorite of American families ever since.

For many years, the Golden was second only to the Labrador Retriever in AKC registrations. In 2007 and 2008, the Golden dropped from second place to fourth place in terms of registration.

Signature Traits The Golden Retriever was bred to retrieve all day long, then get up and do it again the next day. These dogs have incredible stamina, so if you have a Golden, she will not be happy as a lazy lapdog. Mind you, she will love being a lapdog, just not a lazy one.

When it comes to canine intelligence, the Golden Retriever is consistently ranked in the top five. This shouldn't be a surprise, as they were bred to problem solve and think independently in the field. Their superior canine intellect can be a blessing or a curse, depending on your commitment to working with them; intelligent dogs need more training, not less. And although the polls are not scientific, Goldens are consistently named the most affectionate dog!

Breed Standards

Breed standards are important to ensuring the long-term viability of a breed. Without a standard, breeders can breed for traits the public may want but that are not in the best interests of the breed.

Golden Retriever coats can vary in density of undercoat, length, and waviness, and these factors can influence ease of care as well as appearance. If you want to purchase a Golden, select a breeder whose dogs have the kind of coat you desire for your puppy. The same goes for variations in height, head shape, leg bone circumference, body width, and energy level—choose a breeder whose dogs have the features you find desirable, within the scope of the breed standard.

Over the years, small variations in breeding between Europe and the Americas have resulted in two slightly different breed standards, the English and the American.

American Kennel Club—Golden Retriever Breed Standard

General Appearance A symmetrical, powerful, active dog, sound and well put together, not clumsy nor long in the leg, displaying a kindly expression and possessing a personality that is eager, alert, and self-confident. Primarily a hunting dog, he should be shown in hard working condition. Overall appearance, balance, gait, and purpose to be given more emphasis than any of his component parts. *Faults*—Any departure from the described ideal shall be considered faulty to the degree to which it interferes with the breed's purpose or is contrary to breed character.

Size, Proportion, Substance Males 23–24 inches in height at withers; females 21½–22½ inches. Dogs up to one inch above or below standard size should be proportionately penalized. Deviation in height of more than one inch from the standard shall *disqualify*. Length from breastbone to point of buttocks slightly greater than height at withers in ratio of 12:11. Weight for dogs 65–75 pounds; bitches 55–65 pounds.

Head Broad in skull, slightly arched laterally and longitudinally without prominence of frontal bones (forehead) or occipital bones. *Stop* well defined but not abrupt. *Foreface* deep and wide, nearly as long as skull. *Muzzle* straight in profile, blending smooth and strongly into skull; when viewed in profile or from above, slightly deeper and wider at stop than at tip. No heaviness in flews. Removal of whiskers is permitted but not preferred. *Eyes* friendly and intelligent in expression, medium large with dark, close-fitting rims, set well apart and reasonably deep in sockets. Color preferably dark brown; medium brown acceptable. Slant eyes and narrow, triangular eyes detract from correct expression and are to be faulted. No white or haw visible when looking straight ahead. Dogs showing evidence of functional abnormality of eyelids or eyelashes (such as, but not limited to, trichiasis, entropion, ectropion, or distichiasis) are to be excused from the ring. *Ears* rather short with front edge attached well behind and just above the eye and falling close to cheek. When pulled forward, tip of ear should just cover the eye. Low, hound-like ear set to be faulted. *Nose* black or brownish black, though fading to a lighter shade in cold weather not serious. Pink nose or one seriously lacking in pigmentation to be faulted. *Teeth* scissors bite,

Breed Truths

The list of Golden Retriever champions can, and does, fill a book. Not surprisingly, Goldens have won the Obedience Trial Championship more than any other breed.

in which the outer side of the lower incisors touches the inner side of the upper incisors. Undershot or overshot bite is a *disqualification*. Misalignment of teeth (irregular placement of incisors) or a level bite (incisors meet each other edge to edge) is undesirable, but not to be confused with undershot or overshot. Full dentition. Obvious gaps are serious faults.

Neck, Topline, Body Neck medium long, merging gradually into well laid back shoulders, giving sturdy, muscular appearance. No throatiness. *Backline* strong and level from withers to slightly sloping croup, whether standing or moving. Sloping backline, roach or sway back, flat or steep croup to be faulted. *Body* well balanced, short coupled, deep through the chest. *Chest* between forelegs at least as wide as a man's closed hand including thumb, with well developed forechest. Brisket extends to elbow. *Ribs* long and well sprung but not barrel shaped, extending well toward hindquarters. *Loin* short, muscular, wide and deep, with very little tuck-up. Slabsidedness, narrow chest, lack of depth in brisket, excessive tuck-up to be faulted. *Tail* well set on, thick and muscular at the base, following the natural line of the croup. Tail bones extend to, but not below, the point of hock. Carried with merry action, level or with some moderate upward curve; never curled over back nor between legs.

Forequarters Muscular, well coordinated with hindquarters and capable of free movement. *Shoulder blades* long and well laid back with upper tips fairly close together at withers. *Upper arms* appear about the same length as the blades, setting the elbows back beneath the upper tip of the blades, close to the ribs without looseness. *Legs,* viewed from the front, straight with good bone, but not to the point of coarseness. *Pasterns* short and strong, sloping slightly with no suggestion of weakness. Dewclaws on forelegs may be removed, but are normally left on. **Feet** medium size, round, compact, and well knuckled, with thick pads. Excess hair may be trimmed to show natural size and contour. Splayed or hare feet to be faulted.

Hindquarters Broad and strongly muscled. Profile of croup slopes slightly; the pelvic bone slopes at a slightly greater angle (approximately 30 degrees from horizontal). In a natural stance, the femur joins the pelvis at approximately a 90-degree angle; *stifles* well bent; *hocks* well let down with short, strong *rear pasterns. Feet* as in front. *Legs* straight when viewed from rear. Cow-hocks, spread hocks, and sickle hocks to be faulted.

Coat Dense and water-repellent with good undercoat. Outer coat firm and resilient, neither coarse nor silky, lying close to body; may be straight or wavy. Untrimmed natural ruff; moderate feathering on back of forelegs and on underbody; heavier feathering on front of neck, back of thighs, and underside of tail. Coat on head, paws, and front of legs is short and even. Excessive length, open coats, and limp, soft coats are very undesirable. Feet may be trimmed and stray hairs neatened, but the natural appearance of coat or outline should not be altered by cutting or clipping.

Color Rich, lustrous golden of various shades. Feathering may be lighter than rest of coat. With the exception of graying or whitening of face or body due to age, any white marking, other than a few white hairs on the chest, should be penalized according to its extent. Allowable light shadings are not to be confused with white markings. Predominant body color which is either extremely pale or extremely dark is undesirable. Some latitude should be given to the light puppy whose coloring shows promise of deepening with maturity. Any noticeable area of black or other off-color hair is a serious fault.

Gait When trotting, gait is free, smooth, powerful, and well coordinated, showing good reach. Viewed from any position, legs turn neither in nor out, nor do feet cross or interfere with each other. As speed increases, feet tend to converge toward center line of balance. It is recommended that dogs be shown on a loose lead to reflect true gait.

Temperament Friendly, reliable, and trustworthy. Quarrelsomeness or hostility toward other dogs or people in normal situations, or an unwarranted show of timidity or nervousness, is not in keeping with Golden Retriever character. Such actions should be penalized according to their significance.

Breed Truths

Breed Standards Are Important

You may see Goldens of varying sizes and colors, and there is room for slight variations within the two breed standards, but radical deviations from the standards should be viewed with suspicion. Goldens are not meant to be 100-pound (45 kg) dogs, nor are they supposed to have pure white coats. If you want a dog with features outside of the breed standards, you may want to consider another breed that has those traits. Breeders who are not true to the breed standards should be avoided; they do not have the best interests of the breed as their primary motivation, and they cannot be trusted to be good custodians of health and temperament, both of which are critical to Golden Retriever breeding.

Disqualifications *Deviation in height of more than one inch from standard either way.*

Undershot or overshot bite.

Kennel Club—Retriever (Golden) Breed Standard

A Breed Standard is the guideline which describes the ideal characteristics, temperament and appearance of a breed and ensures that the breed is fit for function. Absolute soundness is essential. Breeders and judges should at all times be careful to avoid obvious conditions or exaggerations which would be detrimental in any way to the health, welfare or soundness of this breed. From time to time certain conditions or exaggerations may be considered to have the potential to affect dogs in some breeds adversely, and judges and breeders are requested to refer to the Kennel Club website for details of any such current issues. If a feature or quality is desirable it should only be present in the right measure.

General Appearance Symmetrical, balanced, active, powerful, level mover; sound with kindly expression.

Characteristics Biddable, intelligent and possessing natural working ability.

Temperament Kindly, friendly and confident.

Head and Skull Balanced and well chiselled, skull broad without coarseness; well set on neck, muzzle powerful, wide and deep. Length of foreface approximately equals length from well defined stop to occiput. Nose preferably black.

Eyes Dark brown, set well apart, dark rims.

Ears Moderate size, set on approximate level with eyes.

Mouth Jaws strong, with a perfect, regular and complete scissor bite, i.e. upper teeth closely overlapping lower teeth and set square to the jaws.

Neck Good length, clean and muscular.

Forequarters Forelegs straight with good bone, shoulders well laid back, long in blade with upper arm of equal length placing legs well under body. Elbows close fitting.

Body Balanced, short-coupled, deep through heart. Ribs deep, well sprung. Level topline.

Hindquarters Loin and legs strong and muscular, good second thighs, well bent stifles. Hocks well let down, straight when viewed from rear, neither turning in nor out. Cow-hocks highly undesirable.

Feet Round and cat-like.

Tail Set on and carried level with back, reaching to hocks, without curl at tip.

Gait/Movement Powerful with good drive. Straight and true in front and rear. Stride long and free with no sign of hackney action in front.

Coat Flat or wavy with good feathering, dense water-resisting undercoat.

Colour Any shade of gold or cream, neither red nor mahogany. A few white hairs on chest only, permissible.

Size Height at withers: dogs: 56–61 cms (22–24 ins); bitches: 51–56 cms (20–22 ins).

Faults Any departure from the foregoing points should be considered a fault and the seriousness with which the fault should be regarded should be in exact proportion to its degree and its effect upon the health and welfare of the dog, and on the dog's ability to perform its traditional work.

Note Male animals should have two apparently normal testicles fully descended into the scrotum.

© *Copyright The Kennel Club*
Reproduced with their permission.

So what are the primary differences between British and North American Goldens? The British Goldens have a blockier head with a wider, shorter muzzle. Overall, they appear stockier than their North American cousins. Also, the range of colors for the British Goldens tends to be lighter than for the North Americans.

Over time, specialized breeding has created some variations in Goldens within the breed standards. For example, hunting Goldens tend to be lighter boned and have a finer body type than Goldens bred for the show ring. Goldens bred for showing have thicker, heavier bones and a denser coat, both traits being detrimental to a hunting dog. Also, the darker coat of the hunting Goldens provides better camouflage in the field.

Goldens Today

Today, you would be hard pressed to find another breed with the diversity of talents possessed by the Golden Retriever. They can still be found in the field retrieving game for hunters, but they are more often found doing the new work of dogs in the modern age, as therapy dogs, guide dogs, and assistance dogs, participating in search and rescue, as well as a wide variety of sporting events! Did you know that you can even compete in a dance competition with your Golden? No matter what the work, Goldens apply themselves with enthusiasm, winning hearts, and finding new fans at every turn.

Fun Facts

Celebrities and Their Goldens

Over the years, Goldens have found themselves in the spotlight along with their famous owners.

Oprah Winfrey	Gracie, Layla, and Luke
Ronald Regan	Victory
Nick Jonas	Elvis
Matt Lauer	Walden
Mary Tyler Moore	Shadow
Dean Koontz	Trixie
Joan Rivers	Callie
Phyllis Diller	Gemina
Neil Diamond	Sol and Golden Lady
Shawn Johnson	Tucker
Bill Murray	Bark
Jimmy Buffett	Cheeseburger
Anderson Cooper	Ozzie
Bob Newhart	Freddie
Gerald Ford	Liberty and her pup Misty
Morley Safer	Dora
Betty White	Kitta
Ashton Kutcher	Mr. Bojangles
Jane Seymour	Crispin

Chapter Two

The Mind of the Golden Retriever

Too many hunting breeds, including the Golden Retriever, end up in shelters and rescues because their owners don't understand, and work with, the inherent drives bred into their dogs. If you understand how your Golden's mind works and what instincts drive her, then you are on your way to a fabulous relationship with an amazing dog.

A Dog First

Your Golden Retriever is first and foremost, a dog who thinks and reasons like a dog. It is critical you understand how she perceives the world and her role in it. In her world, there is a very clear hierarchy of rank within the pack, and her position within it dictates her behavior. If you have limited or no experience with dogs, I highly recommend reading Jan Fennell's *The Dog Listener*, Patricia McConnell's *The Other End of the Leash,* or Cesar Milan's *Cesar's Way.* While the training methodologies may differ somewhat, each of these books gives the reader a deep insight into how your Golden Retriever thinks, how she interprets her world, and, as a result, why she behaves as she does. More importantly, you learn how you need to behave in order to be an effective leader for you Golden. Why is this important? Because if you do not fill the leadership role in the hierarchy of the pack, your Golden will, and it will cause her no end of stress and give you a headache dealing with the resulting behavioral issues. While she may be equipped to lead a pack of dogs in the wild, she is, without a doubt, wholly incapable of making life decisions for the pack (you and your family) in the human world. And that is exactly what she will try to do if you do not step up and lead.

Your Golden Talks to You

Your Golden talks to you and other dogs all the time using the language of canines, her body. If you pay attention and study canine body language, it will help you to understand her when she is communicating with you. (My favorite book on this subject can be found in the Resources section.)

FYI: A Touch from a Stranger

To your Golden, a pat on the head is like a hug; it is okay from her family, but uncomfortable from a stranger. If strangers ask to pet your Golden, tell them to pat her either on her back or under her chin.

The Working Dog

Unlike other breeds whose long-term popularity has bred back many of their original working traits, the Golden Retriever has spent more years in the hunting field than in the living room. Up until the 1960s, most Golden Retrievers were chosen and bred for their skill in the field. This required a dog with a quick mind, a biddable temperament, a soft mouth, a keen nose, attentive behavior, and the ability to not only remain quiet for hours in a duck blind, but to think for herself when far afield from her handler.

Your Golden Retriever is not going to be satisfied with a life as a lapdog. (However, she will love to curl herself up on your lap at the first hint of an invitation!) She needs to have some kind of job. Now, this can be as simple as fetching the morning paper, bringing her leash to you for walks, carrying a basket back from the market, or picking up the kids' toys and putting them in a basket. Do you notice a common element in all of these activities? Yes, they all relate to her retrieval instinct. Her retrieval instinct is powerful, and if not properly channeled, it will make you crazy! (Think dirty underwear proudly trotted out to show your dinner guests.) Trust me, you want and need a positive channel for this powerful drive.

Goldens Are Not Kennel Dogs

Unlike some other breeds of hunting dogs, Golden Retrievers do not do well in a kennel environment. Because Goldens are so focused on their own-

Breed Needs

Goldens Must Work

Your Golden Retriever is an energetic, highly intelligent dog who was bred to work, which means she needs to be mentally and physically challenged. These needs must be met in order to keep her from getting into mischief born of boredom and pent-up energy. Making sure she has plenty of exercise and a purpose will keep her, and you, happy and content, and it will also strengthen the bond between you and you Golden. It may be as simple as bringing in the newspaper at the end of your walk in the morning, or as challenging as rally or agility competitions, but your Golden needs to have some sort of work in her life, and it is better if that work is directed by you rather than something she creates on her own.

ers, they do best in a home setting with access to their human companions. As far as your Golden is concerned, home with you is where her heart is.

Goldens Are Not Good Guard Dogs

For all their talents, one thing Golden Retrievers do not excel at is being guard dogs. With their cheerful, easygoing personality, they are more likely to lead the thief to Grandma's silver in exchange for a treat or a toss of the tennis ball. Your Golden may bark when someone new comes around, but don't count on her to scare anyone off.

Getting to Know Goldens

Tuned In, in High Definition

"She watches me all the time! It makes me crazy!" Because they are bred to work as part of a team, Golden Retrievers are hardwired to closely watch their handlers for signals and directions This readiness and vigilant attentiveness to their handlers is what makes Golden Retrievers exceptional hunting dogs. It is important to understand the origins of your Golden's watchfulness, so that you don't misinterpret it as neediness. She isn't needy, she is just ready; there's a big difference. (In Chapter 7, we will discuss how to make the most of this instinctive watchfulness.) She will also follow you from room to room—again, not because she is needy, but rather because she is ready.

The Truth About Intelligence

The Golden Retriever is ranked in the top five for canine intelligence. Depending on your approach, this can be a blessing or a curse. Contrary to popular belief, a highly intelligent dog such as the Golden requires more training than the average dog. Why? The Golden's very active mind will become bored if she doesn't get adequate mental stimulation. Remember, these dogs were bred to problem solve in the field. When obedience training is done for the day, be prepared to move on to games that force her to think. A simple game of fetch is not going to be enough. Work with her innate instincts and create games where she has to search out and retrieve her toys and treats.

This is a character trait you will need to think long and hard about before you bring a Golden into your home. Why is it important for you to be aware of this? Well, first of all, indulging what can be incorrectly perceived as neediness can create a host of behavioral issues. Second, continually reprimanding her for instinctual behavior will create behavioral problems. Third, being constantly watched and followed is not comfortable for some people.

Goldens also have an incredible intuitive nature, which makes them exceptional therapy dogs. Their ability to pick up on emotions and provide the proper response is astonishing. A well-placed snuggle is often just what

the doctor ordered to relieve pain, both physical and emotional. And a head on your lap after a long, hard day brings much-needed stress relief.

Nosey, Nosey, Nosey!

Your Golden Retriever is bred to have a keen nose and an inquisitive nature, so she is nosey on two fronts. In the field, Goldens search out game in order to flush it for the hunter, then, using their nose again, locate the downed bird and retrieve it. Hunting is the biggest thrill a Golden can experience, even if the hunt is for that particularly stinky pair of socks at the bottom of the laundry basket.

If you don't train her not to sniff everything, walking with your Golden can present a bit of a challenge, as she will try to investigate every smell that tickles her olfactory system.

Mouthy, Mouthy, Mouthy!

You would be hard pressed to find a mouthier dog than the Golden Retriever. Her instinct to pick things up and bring them to you is hardwired into her brain. What does this mean for you? Until she is trained, your Golden is going to pick up everything!

Fun Facts

Oh, That Retrieval Instinct!

Louise Dobbe, of the rescue group Retrieve a Golden of Minnesota (RAGOM), told me a hilarious story about her beloved rescue Golden, Mike. It was Mike's habit to bring the morning newspaper in after his walk. One day, Mike decided that if one paper made Mom and Dad happy, then they would be overjoyed with three or four! So he set about retrieving the neighbors' newspapers and delivering them to Louise and her husband. Needless to say, Louise and her neighbors got a good laugh as she returned the slightly damp, and somewhat tardy, newspapers!

PERSONALITY POINTERS
Golden Retriever Body Language

Mood	Friendly (without excitement)	Curious	Playful
Head Carriage	Normal head position or slightly lowered.	Normal posture and head position. Sometimes tilted toward the item of interest.	"Play bow," chest and head lowered to ground, head looking up.
Eyes	Open and soft. She may make tension-free direct eye contact if she knows you. A more timid Golden may squint and blink as well.	Open, with a possible furrowed brow. Aligned with the nose toward the item of interest.	Squinty eyes, denoting team-work.
Ears	Relaxed	Up and alert.	Up and alert.
Mouth	Closed or slightly open in a "smile." The lips are without tension.	May be either open or closed, but in either case, the lips are without tension.	Closed or slightly open, but without any tension in the lips.
Body	Relaxed posture and movements.	Usually a more forward position, to get closer but safely. If she can, she will paw at the item of interest to inspect it more closely.	Chest lowered to ground, elbows close to or touching the ground, rump elevated. This is the classic "play bow."
Tail	Gently wagging, straight out from her body.	If the item doesn't generate any fear, the tail will likely be wagging or straight out.	In "play bow" the tail is lowered, but wagging.
Voice	Generally quiet. Sometimes a happy whimper may escape.	Generally silent.	Vocalizations vary. Sharp, short invitation barks, growling or odd variations of growling, all designed to encourage play.

Apprehensive or anxious	Fearful	Ready to work!
Neck stiff, head may be pulled back slightly.	Head slightly lowered, sometimes turned in submission.	Head slightly forward and raised.
Wide open, may appear bug-eyed, whites of eyes may show, may have fixed stare. Her eyes follow the source of the anxiety, but her nose is pointed away from it. Eye contact is avoided.	Eyes wide, whites of eyes may show—this is known as whale eye. She may also squint her eyes. In either case, her eyes will be averted.	Eyes alternate between looking at you and looking toward either the car or the activity at hand.
Pulled back.	Ears pulled back or flattened against skull.	Alert and forward.
Closed or slightly open. She may yawn even though she isn't tired.	Slightly open, teeth may be visible, may be drooling.	Open, possibly panting with anticipation.
Tense and somewhat rigid. Back may be rounded. Front legs are braced and a paw may be lifted, a prelude to fleeing.	Tense and/or trembling, she will try to get close to you or a wall. Her back may be rounded and her body somewhat twisted in a submissive posture.	Rigid, with a forward cant to her posture; she may be dancing in circles!
Partially lowered to tucked under.	Lowered between legs or curled up toward the belly.	Straight out, or wagging like a flag in a hurricane!
Generally silent.	Can vary from silent to whimpering or actual crying.	Generally silent, though happy barks may escape.

But also, as you will see in Chapter 4, it makes teaching your young puppy not to nip and bite fairly simple.

Given the opportunity, Golden Retrievers can be brilliant thieves. Be sure to read and learn the training commands *leave it* and *give/drop* in Chapter 7 and *give* in Chapter 10.

The Training Conundrum

Because of her natural exuberance, it may take longer to train your Golden Retriever, but she is eager to be taught and has an amazing ability to retain and recall all she has learned, both the good and the bad. What does this mean for you? If she learns or teaches herself bad habits, it will take a while to retrain her. Your diligence in making sure the lessons her incredible mind retains are good lessons will pay huge dividends.

Breed Truths

The One-Handler Dog

In the field, the Labrador Retriever is generally willing to work for multiple handlers. Not so the Golden Retriever. The Golden is wholly focused on her handler and only her handler.

Forever Young Golden Retrievers are generally slow to mature and usually retain their playfulness for their entire lifetime. While she may be physically mature, your Golden is not going to move out of her puppyhood until she is two to three years old, which is why training is so critical. A full-grown, out-of-control Golden is a disaster waiting to happen.

Problem Solver One of the key traits that makes Golden Retrievers such valuable dogs in the field is their ability to problem solve. While most dogs will simply repeat what they have been trained to do, the Golden Retriever will figure out the best way to do it and improve upon her training—yet another reason to make sure the lessons your Golden learns are good ones.

Your Golden works very hard to understand you and what you want from her. She will cock her head to one side and study you. She lives to please you. Reward her by making the same commitment to understanding her. The happiest times in your Golden Retriever's life, and yours, will be those moments when you two connect, somewhere in that place where the human and canine minds meet and understand each other. It is magic.

Communicating with Your Golden Retriever____

Voice   The tone and cadence of your words, as well as the words themselves, have a significant impact on your Golden Retriever. Unlike her cousin, the Labrador Retriever, who can bounce back from harsh words and tone, your Golden has a sensitive nature, and harsh, angry words will have a long-term, negative effect on her. It is critical that you exercise patience when talking to her, even if she is having a "moment" and is making you crazy. Keep your tone low and the cadence of your voice slow. Low and slow presents a departure from your normal speaking voice, so she will know you are addressing her, and it will offer her a level of verbal reassurance. Words spoken low and slow have a calming effect, and they are often the best way to temper her natural exuberance.

Your Golden has her own voice in the form of her bark or whine. Over time, you will be able to discern the difference between "Watch out! Here comes a scary person whom we don't know!" and "Oh boy! Here is my favorite UPS driver!" She will also tell you when her joy at seeing you is beyond expression by a little whine accompanied by her happy dance.

Hands   Since dogs naturally communicate with each other through body movement, it is very easy to add hand signals to your training commands. In fact, it may make your training easier because you are speaking the same physical language. Hand signals make working with your Golden from a distance much easier, and they also exercise her mind, which is important. Many activities, such as hunting, agility, competitive obedience, and freestyle dancing, require hand signals for communicating with your Golden.

One of the most compelling reasons for teaching your Golden hand signals is to make her senior years easier. Most dogs, like humans, begin to lose their hearing as they age. If you have taught your Golden hand signals, adjusting to hearing loss will be appreciably easier on both her and you.

Facial Expressions   Your Golden's face can be a landscape of emotions! Relaxed lips and ears, and a closed or marginally open mouth, along with a soft expression in her eyes, will tell you that she is in a relaxed and happy mood. Conversely, a furrowed brow, eyes wide open, ears back, and mouth open with the lips drawn back are all signs that your Golden is experiencing some level of tension and discomfort in her current circumstances. As your relationship grows, so will your understanding of her facial expressions. And yes, dogs do smile!

As you read her expressions, she is also reading yours. Be sure to smile when she is a good girl and try not to laugh when you have to correct her for something goofy. Telling her *No* with a happy look on your face will confuse her. When you do need to correct her, try to keep your face neutral rather than angry. Remember, she is very sensitive, and even if your voice does not reflect the anger, if she reads it in your face, she will be affected by it.

Body Movement

Body movement is the primary form of canine communication. A dog leaning forward, with a stiff posture and laid back ears, is asserting herself, whereas a dog whose front elbows are on the ground, with hind end up in the air and tail waving like a flag on a windy day, is performing the classic play bow. Is her tail tucked between her legs? This means she is fearful. I encourage you to become a student of canine body language, because it gives you a great deal of insight into how your Golden is reacting to any given situation.

So what about your body language? First and foremost, never use threatening body language with your Golden. Don't loom over her in a stiff and urgent manner, or ever raise your hand or leg as if to do her harm. You will damage her spirit, and it will forever affect your relationship with her. However, it is wonderful to leap and run with her when she has mastered a new skill, or give the couch an inviting pat so that she can hop up and snuggle. She will spend her entire life watching you, reading you, trying to understand you; be sure to send her the right messages.

Scents

Since they were bred to search out game, Golden Retrievers have a highly developed sense of smell. Your Golden perceives her world in large part through her nose, which can make walks in a new area a bit of challenge. While posture gives dogs some information, we are all too familiar with the quintessential canine butt sniff. Not only is it a form of greeting, it is also an information-gathering session on the overall health and vitality of the other dog. When you come home from work, she may take a cursory sniff as you walk through the door, recognize the daily smells of your workplace, and then stop sniffing. However, she will give you a thorough sniffing when you come back from your friend's house, where there were not only new people, but a cat and a dog as well. Now you are completely fascinating to her, and she will not rest until her curiosity is fully satisfied.

Chapter Three

How to Choose a Golden Retriever

F inding the right Golden Retriever for you and your family requires research and resolve, but the rewards are worth all of the effort. Having a happy, healthy, well-adjusted Golden in your home is pure joy—most of the time. Any Golden owner can regale you with stories of the mischief Golden's can get into; however, that curious nature and boundless zest for life, which sometimes lead to mischief, are also a big part of why these dogs are so near and dear to our hearts. They give us unconditional love and devotion, all the while keeping us laughing and shaking our heads at the same time. It doesn't get any better than that!

Is a Golden Retriever Right for You?

The first step in choosing a Golden Retriever is to evaluate whether your, family and lifestyle are suited for a Golden. Goldens are fantastic dogs, but they are definitely not for everyone. (If you haven't already, go back and read Chapter 2).

Here are some questions to ask yourself and your family:

- First and foremost, are you willing to make a commitment to care for a Golden for her entire life, which can be a dozen years or longer?
- Will you be willing to adjust your lifestyle when your aging Golden begins to slow down?
- Are you willing to make the financial commitment that comes with owning a large dog of a breed that is prone to several genetic issues?
- Are you willing to take the time to train your Golden beyond just one puppy class and a Level One obedience class? The well-behaved Golden who lives down the street didn't come that way; she is the product of dedicated owners who are committed to her training.
- Are you willing to lock up the laundry and anything else a mouthy Golden may get into and chew or, worse yet, swallow? Having a Golden will make you a better housekeeper.
- Are you willing to keep your counters clear of food, or your Golden out of the kitchen when needed? The roast you put on the counter to rest is

good game to a Golden, whose hunting instincts make her a notorious counter surfer!

- Are you willing to tail-proof your house? Those beautiful Golden tail plumes are great coffee table dusters and will swat that crystal vase right off along with the dust.
- Are you willing to make schedule changes in your life, so that your Golden isn't left alone for long periods of time? Goldens don't do well when left alone for hours on end; because they are bred to be part of a working team, they are focused on being with you, not the washer and dryer in the laundry room. A puppy will need to have potty breaks during the day, but an adult can be left the span of a normal workday, at most. A Golden who is left alone too much can develop behavioral issues.
- You do understand Goldens make lousy guard dogs, right? Everyone is a friend to a Golden, whether they have come to dinner or to take the silver.
- Are you okay with a slimy, soggy tennis ball being dropped in your lap as an invitation to play? Will you accept the invitation and go and have some fun with your Golden?
- Do you understand and accept that Golden Retrievers are slow to mature, which means you will have a large, enthusiastic puppy for a couple of years?

COMPATIBILITY Is the Golden Retriever the Best Breed for You?

ENERGY LEVEL	• • • •
EXERCISE REQUIREMENTS	• • • •
PLAYFULNESS	• • • •
AFFECTION LEVEL	• • • •
FRIENDLINESS TOWARD OTHER PETS	• • •
FRIENDLINESS TOWARD STRANGERS	• • •
FRIENDLINESS TOWARD CHILDREN	• • •
EASE OF TRAINING	• •
GROOMING REQUIREMENTS	• •
SHEDDING	• • • •
SPACE REQUIREMENTS	• • •
OK FOR BEGINNERS	• • • •

4 dots = highest rating

- Are you willing to exercise your Golden, regardless of the weather, every day? What about multiple times a day? And I don't mean just a quick trip around the block—Goldens require vigorous exercise. Remember, they were bred to work in the field all day long, day after day.
- Goldens shed a lot! Are you a pro with the vacuum cleaner and lint brush?
- Do you like brushing a dog? Every week or every day during high shedding periods? Goldens require regular brushing and combing.
- Are you okay with a stray dog hair in your food? Will you just pick it out and continue eating? You will be amazed where those golden hairs can float to!
- Is everyone in your home free of dog allergies? Goldens are not allergy friendly. If someone in your home is allergic to dogs, a Golden Retriever will cause an allergic reaction.
- Are you okay with dirt, mud, and water? Are you okay with it on the floors, on the furniture, on the walls, on your clothes, or on the ceiling if she shakes before you can grab the towel and clean her up? Goldens love water, and like to dig, and if they can dig in a puddle and come up with mud, well, that's a Golden's happy place.
- Are you okay with big, sloppy dog kisses? Or with a big, lovable dog crawling onto your lap for a nighttime snuggle?
- Do you live to come home to your dog, whose whole world revolves around you? Are you willing to fall in love and make a commitment for her lifetime?

If you answered *"no"* to any of these questions, stop and think long and hard about proceeding with the purchase of a Golden Retriever. While some of this list was written tongue in cheek, there is real truth behind every point. Golden Retrievers are marvelous dogs; however, too many end up in shelters and rescue organizations, because their owners did not understand the breed and what adding a Golden to their family would entail.

If you answered *"yes"* to all of these questions, let's take a look at what you need to do to get the best Golden possible for you and your family!

A Healthy Pedigree

The health of your Golden's parents and siblings has a profound impact on the health of your dog. The health issues common to Golden Retrievers are either directly inherited or endemic to the breed.

The GRCA recommends that dogs should not be bred until they are two years old and have reached physical and mental maturity. Dogs chosen for breeding should have the typical Golden Retriever temperament, be in good health, and have examination reports for the following health issues: hip dysplasia, elbow dysplasia, hereditary eye diseases, and cardiovascular disease. Breeders should register the test results of their breeding dogs and resulting progeny with the Canine Health Information Center (CHIC), a centralized canine health database sponsored

Never, Ever Buy on Impulse

All Golden puppies are cute, every last one of them! However, not all Golden puppies are bred to have the good health and temperament you want in a first-rate family companion or working dog. As you will learn in Chapter 6, Golden Retrievers, unfortunately, have numerous genetic issues that are endemic to the breed. Unreliable temperaments are also an issue within the breed due to irresponsible breeding. The good news is that with proper breeding many, if not most, of these issues can be avoided. Why is this important to you? Because ignorance is not bliss when it comes to your Golden's family history and breeding. Ignorance of your Golden's lineage and her health history can quickly turn into an emotional and financial nightmare.

Please read the rest of this chapter very carefully. If you cannot get a documented pedigree, with accepted health test results on all of the parent dogs going back at least three generations, do not buy the puppy—just walk away. Why? Because the potential long-term emotional and financial costs could be overwhelming, as there's a slim chance of you getting a healthy puppy. What you think you are saving on the initial price of the puppy will pale in comparison to the short- and long-term veterinary costs. If you truly want to add a Golden Retriever to your family, take the time and do the research needed to find a reputable breeder. It will pay huge dividends, with the sweet result of your efforts being a happy, healthy puppy for you and your family.

by the AKC/Canine Health Foundation (AKC/CHF) and the Orthopedic Foundation for Animals (OFA). In order to meet the GRCA's basic standards, a Golden should have normal results on a CHIC certificate. You can verify the CHIC status by using the searchable online database listed in the Resources section.

Sibling data, or vertical pedigree data, are also available in the CHIC database. Vertical pedigree data are often a better predictor of health than parental data alone, because they indicate the range of possibilities for health or disease in the four CHIC categories. For more information on vertical pedigrees and how they can be a useful predictor of health, see the Resources section.

Finding and Evaluating a Breeder

I agree wholeheartedly with the GRCA that your best resource for a Golden Retriever is a serious hobby breeder who's in it for the love and betterment of the breed, not for the money. In fact, most serious hobby breeders don't expect to make a profit; it's a labor of love.

The best way to locate a reputable breeder is to make inquiries with the local Golden Retriever club in your area. Any good breeder will be a member of the GRCA, the local Golden Retriever club, or an all-breed club. In a perfect world, he or she will belong to all three and will be committed to

following the code of ethics outlined by each organization. You can also attend AKC- and GRCA- sponsored events and inquire about breeders with the people competing with their Goldens—especially the winners!

If you're simply looking for a family companion, a breeder focused on show dogs, who traditionally have a mellower temperament, may be a better choice than one focused on breeding hunting Goldens, who have a much more intense drive. Within a litter of puppies, some are selected for competition, and those who are not competition quality are sold at a pet price rather than at show dog prices. And the great thing is that these puppies have received the same careful breeding and nurturing that went into their show-worthy siblings.

Here is a list of questions and things to look for when evaluating a breeder:

- Does the breeder participate in GRCA health studies and does he or she encourage puppy owners to

Helpful Hints

The AKC and the GRCA

It is a common misconception that the designation "AKC" or "AKC Papers" is a guarantee of quality. It is not. The AKC (American Kennel Club) is a registry body, and the AKC designation only means that the dog is a purebreed. Within the AKC, there are Parent Clubs for each breed, and the national club for Goldens is the GRCA (Golden Retriever Club of America). It is the GRCA Code of Ethics that dictates the principles to which all Golden Retriever breeders should adhere.

do the same? This indicates a true commitment to the betterment of the breed.

- Are all of the sire and dam's health certificates registered and available online with the CHIC?
- Does he or she feed the puppies on a "slow-grow plan" for long-term health? Will he or she give you the details of the diet so that you can continue it at home?
- Is the litter registered with the AKC?
- Will the AKC registration application, with the breeder's section filled out, be given to you when you pick up your puppy? Will a three- to five-generation pedigree accompany it? Will the puppy's vaccination and medical records be given to you at the time of pickup?
- Are you permitted to visit the property? Is it clean and do all of the puppies appear healthy and well-socialized to both dogs and people? Does the dam appear to have a good temperament?
- Does the breeder specialize in a particular type of Golden? For example, is he or she focused on producing show-quality Goldens or hunting Goldens?
- Does the breeder provide references not only from people who have purchased puppies, but from other breeders and from the veterinarian who provides care for the breeder's dogs?
- Does the breeder actively compete with his or her Goldens in the sport of choice? While all dogs aren't champions, a breeder who competes will breed and nurture all of the puppies as if they were, both for the love of his or her Goldens, and to maintain a good reputation.
- Does the breeder provide a contract and health guarantee?

What to Expect from a Breeder

Just as you expect to buy a high-quality puppy from a top-notch breeder, the breeder should expect to sell only to a reliable caretaker, who will bring the puppy into a loving home and provide for the physical and emotional needs of a Golden Retriever. You should feel like you are being interviewed by the breeder for the privilege of taking home one of the puppies. And bringing home a well-bred Golden Retriever is a privilege—and a joy! The breeder should ask very specific questions in order to learn how you plan to care for the puppy and if you intend to work or compete with her. Some potential questions you may be asked are

- Why do you want a Golden Retriever?
- Have you ever owned or trained a dog before?
- Where will your puppy sleep?
- How many hours will she be left alone each day?
- What will you feed her?

These questions are your indication that the breeder is sincerely concerned about the puppy's well-being. Remember, this is a breeder committed to the well-being of every one of the dogs. He or she also knows the dogs, and, if your plan is to have a layabout Golden, he or she will be able to tell you whether or not one of the dogs can fill that role.

Don't be surprised if you are asked to remove your shoes before being allowed in the puppy area at the breeder's facility. The puppies are too young to be fully vaccinated, and shoes carry potentially deadly pathogens, such as parvovirus. Understandably, many breeders will not allow visitation until the puppies are nearly ready to go home.

After purchasing your Golden Retriever puppy, the breeder should encourage you to call with any questions or concerns. In fact, he or she should insist on it. This shows the breeder cares about the puppies and is making a proactive effort to improve the quality of future litters. The breeder should also require your contact information so he or she can get in touch with you, most likely to check on the puppy's progress and to request periodic photos. Chances are good, he or she is missing her pups!

Will Your Golden Have a Job?

If you plan to work your Golden in some capacity, be it hunting, showing, or any other job or sport at which Goldens excel, it is wise to locate a breeder who specializes in breeding Goldens for that purpose. Why? Well, to begin with, these breeders have a great deal of experience, knowing what traits need to be accentuated in order for a dog to excel at a particular job; they can breed, within the standard, to emphasize those traits. They can also begin conditioning pups before they leave their homes. For example, a breeder who specializes in hunting Goldens will breed to the smaller, lighter side of the standard because these dogs do better in the field. The breeder may also actively hunt his or her Goldens, as well as compete in various field trials. A breeder of hunting Goldens can selectively breed the traits necessary to make them exceptional in the field—namely, a steady, focused temperament, so as to remain calm during close range gunfire, a strong-willed personality with a high level of intensity and energy, a keen nose, and high intelligence. A breeder of hunting Goldens will likely begin to teach and condition the litter for field skills.

Breed Needs

Golden Rescue

Like dogs of every breed, some Golden Retrievers don't have a happy beginning to their lives and need to be rehomed or rescued from bad situations. And sadly, many great dogs are let go by their families due to changes in family circumstances. These dogs are all looking for a new forever home. Fortunately, there are many Golden rescue organizations around the country. Consider a rescue when thinking about bringing a Golden into your home.

BE PREPARED! Breeder Red Flags

Unfortunately, you may run into a few unscrupulous breeders in your search. Here are some red flags to watch out for:

- The breeder doesn't want you to visit the property to meet the sire and dam or to pick up your puppy.
- Be wary of a USDA license, as this is generally not needed by a hobby breeder and may indicate a large-scale breeding operation.
- The breeder allows the puppies to leave before they are eight weeks of age.
- The AKC registration application isn't available at the time of puppy pickup and the breeder uses the excuse of "the AKC hasn't sent the papers yet." The AKC processes and returns applications in about three weeks, plenty of time for a responsible, organized breeder to have the papers available for the new owner.
- The breeder seems concerned about how you are going to pay for the pup. It is likely that the breeder is in the breeding business for all the wrong reasons if the main concern is money. Also, hobby breeders generally do not accept credit cards, so this should also raise a red flag.
- The puppies should be clean, well fed, healthy, energetic, and social. If the puppies are dirty and foul smelling, or have glassy eyes or runny noses, you should be apprehensive. And don't forget to check the cleanliness of the ears.
- Is the breeder producing dogs that are outside of the breed standard—for example, 100-pound (45 kg) Goldens or ones whose fur is white? If a breeder is working outside the breed standard, it is unlikely that he or she is conscientious in the realm of health and temperament.
- Is the breeder selling several different breeds of dogs? Selling more than one or two breeds of dogs can often be a sign of a puppy mill or puppy broker. Serious hobby breeders tend to specialize in just one or sometimes two breeds. Only consider a multi-breed breeder if he or she is successfully competing in some venue with each of the breeds.
- Golden Retriever litters require a great deal of time to keep clean, exercised, and well-socialized. And although it is common for females living together to cycle together, thus creating a situation in which a reputable breeder may have more than one litter at a time, more than a couple of litters in a period of several months may stretch a breeder's time and energy too thin to do a good job with the puppies. A breeder with a nearly continuous, year-round supply of puppies may be operating a puppy mill.

If you see evidence of neglect or abuse of either the puppies or the parents, do not hesitate to contact the American Society for the Prevention of Cruelty to Animals (ASPCA) at *www.aspca.org*. Your voice may be the neglected animals only defense.

Each job or sport has breeders who work to produce champions, so take the time to find a breeder who creates champions in your area of interest.

Health Guarantees and Contracts

Make certain that you are able to view, and are given a written copy of, the breeder's guarantee and contract before you send any deposit money. Many breeders and websites claim that they guarantee their puppies but fail to provide you with a written copy, which can lead to confusion regarding what is or isn't covered. If they are reputable breeders and are confident in their puppies, they will be more than happy to provide you with this information before you send them any deposit money. Read the health guarantee and contract very carefully and make sure you are comfortable with all of the terms. For example, if a legitimate genetic defect is found, will you be required to return your puppy to the breeder? Or will the breeder refund a portion of your purchase price to help defray some of the veterinary costs? Or will the breeder help to rehome your puppy, with a full release of her medical records, to another family better able to manage the health issues? What are you as the owner required to do while raising your puppy in order to comply with the terms of the health guarantee? For example, some breeders require that the puppy be fed a specific diet in order for the guarantee to remain valid.

I cannot stress enough the importance of reading and understanding the breeder's health guarantee. As the owner of the puppy, ensure that your interests are covered, not just the interests of the breeder.

Beware of unscrupulous breeders who charge extra for a health guarantee or normal puppy veterinary checks. Again, this is not something reputable breeders do, and you should seriously reconsider getting a puppy from such a breeder.

10 Questions About Adopting a Rescue Golden

1 **Q: Does it make a difference whether I get my rescue Golden from a shelter or from a rescue organization that fosters Goldens in volunteers' homes?**

A: A rescue organization that fosters its dogs with volunteers will be able to match you with a rescued Golden that is well-suited for you and your family. Because they live with the dogs in a home environment, the volunteers have an insight into the personality and idiosyncrasies of the Goldens they foster, which can be very helpful to you. Does this rule out getting a Golden from a shelter? Absolutely not! But if you do, be sure you have access to support and mentoring, so that you can effectively deal with any surprise issues that, as a first-time dog owner, you may not know how to handle.

2 **Q: Why does the rescue organization require a home visit after I fill out the application and questionnaire?**

A: Volunteers who are specially trained in home visits will assess you and your home to decide if both are well suited to a Golden from their organization. The volunteer will talk to every member of the family to make sure everyone is on board with getting a rescue dog. In addition to the family, and house, the yard, fencing, and proximity to busy streets or other hazards will all be assessed.

The rescue organization gleans all of this valuable information from the application and home visit.

3 **Q: If I am giving a Golden a new home, why do I have to pay an adoption fee? What if I can't afford the adoption fee?**

A: Most non-governmental shelters and rescue organizations run on donations and the kindness of volunteers. And as with any operation, there are costs, from office space, copier fees, and mailings to web-hosting fees, so that the public can look at the available dogs online. The biggest expense however is providing some level of veterinary care.

If you cannot afford the adoption fee, sadly, you probably cannot afford the even higher cost of dog ownership.

4 **Q: Our local news recently ran a story about several Goldens rescued from a puppy mill, but when I inquired about adopting one of these dogs, they said I couldn't because I did not have another dog in my home. Why is that important?**

A: The life of a puppy mill dog is beyond sad. Having another dog in the house comforts them and allows them to learn how to be a normal dog by watching the dog who is already living a normal life with good people. In short, the home dog acts as a model for the puppy mill dog. Puppy mill dogs are very shy, and having other dogs around cuts down on their adjustment time—from a year or more without another dog, to six months with a home dog.

5 **Q: I would love to adopt an older Golden, but I am concerned about health issues. Do rescue organizations provide some financial support?**
A: For the most part, no. Rescue organizations run on a shoestring and the kindness of volunteers. Extra funds are seldom, if ever, available. It is generally expected that once you own the dog, you are responsible for her in every way.

6 **Q: Will a rescue make a good therapy dog?**
A: Many rescue Goldens go on to become fabulous therapy dogs. Owners of rescue Goldens who work as therapy teams believe their rescued Goldens have a special understanding of those who feel rejected or abandoned. If therapy work is your intention, be specific about your desire to do this when you talk to the shelter or rescue organization. They will look for a Golden with a personality suited for this type of work.

7 **Q: I feel that I am too old to raise a puppy or to struggle through the teenage phase, but I would still love a rescue Golden. What do you recommend?**
A: There are many older Goldens with a bit of gray on their muzzles who can be a very nice match for the bit of gray in your hair. While your time together may be shorter, you can still enjoy many wonderful years, taking leisurely strolls and happily dozing during the evening news.

8 **Q: I want a dog, but my spouse does not. Would a rescue Golden be easier?**
A: No. It is critical that all members of the household agree to add a Golden to the home. Adopting a dog against the wishes of your spouse will create tension in your home, which will have an adverse effect on your relationship and on your new rescue Golden. Goldens are incredibly sensitive dogs, and the last thing a rescue needs is to be in a home where tensions are high and resentment is focused on her. Instead, become a volunteer to get your Golden "fix."

9 **Q: Our budget is tight, and we think a rescue Golden would be a cheaper way to go. Is this a correct assumption?**
A: No, it could, potentially, be the opposite. Rescue Goldens are seldom perfect, and there are any number of expenses associated with making a Golden perfect for you, especially when her background isn't known. An assessment of finances is needed before you commit to bring a rescue into your home.

10 **Q: We have children. Is a rescue Golden a good option for our family?**
A: It can be. However, it is critical that you know the background of the Golden and if she has successfully lived with children before, particularly young children. Unfortunately, many rescue Goldens have had bad experiences with a child and then generalize that fear and anxiety to all children. Work very closely with your shelter or rescue organization to get a Golden who will be a great companion for your children and not a potential danger.

Chapter Four

Caring for a Golden Retriever Puppy

Caring for your new Golden Retriever begins before you bring her home. You need to decide how you will transport her home; is your breeder close enough for a drive, or will you need to have your puppy shipped by air? Your home and property need to be made safe for a mouthy, curious puppy who is going to stick her nose into everything and try to put a lot of it in her mouth. Various types of puppy gear need to be purchased (and purchased again as she grows), and decisions have to be made about her food, sleeping arrangements, scheduling, potty spots, and who is responsible for her care—not to mention locating a veterinarian and making her first wellness appointment. Phew! And she isn't even home yet! Bringing a new Golden puppy into your home is its own special kind of pandemonium, but by being prepared, you can mitigate some of the chaos.

Transporting Your Puppy Home

As tempting as it may be, do not transport your new Golden Retriever home on your lap. It is best to keep her in a small kennel or carrier secured by a seat belt or a bungee cord. Unrestrained puppies, like children, can become projectiles in an accident or with a sudden stomp on the brakes. On the trip home, expect her to cry… a lot! She has just been taken from everything she knows, so naturally she is scared and lonely. The crying will subside as she gets used to you, your family, and her new surroundings.

Keep her on a leash, preferably attached to a harness rather than a collar, anytime she is not in her travel kennel or carrier. Why a harness? Remember, this sweet little Golden doesn't know you well, and she may try to back away from you, slipping right out of her collar. Trust me, I learned this lesson the hard way, and it is terrifying!

If you travel any distance to get your Golden, avoid rest stops. If she is younger than 16 weeks, your Golden puppy is not fully vaccinated, and

CHECKLIST

Things to Bring When You Pick Up Your Puppy

Traveling home with your new Golden Retriever puppy is less stressful if you are prepared. There is a good chance your puppy will get carsick, need a drink of water or some food, or have to eliminate during the car ride home. And there's no guarantee the elimination or vomiting will happen outside of the car. See where I'm going? Here is a list of things to bring with you on your journey, with my sincere hopes that you won't need some of them.

✔ Her puppy collar (with tags attached), harness, and leash.

✔ A small travel crate or soft-sided carrier.

✔ A travel partner who can drive, while you attend to your new puppy.

✔ One or two chew-safe puppy toys.

✔ A water dish and food bowl.

✔ A clean, empty water jug to fill at the breeder's home.

✔ Enough food to feed her appropriately during the journey. Remember, puppies have to eat every few hours.

✔ A small blanket to wrap your pup in when you hold her.

✔ A roll of paper towels.

✔ A package of puppy wipes.

✔ A package of disinfecting wipes to clean the car and/or her carrier.

✔ Large puppy piddle pads or paper tablecloths for use during potty stops.

✔ A trash bag or two in case there are no public trash cans available.

✔ A cheerful, patient attitude!

Remember, traveling home with you is going to be stressful for the wee puppy, so knowing things may not go smoothly—and being prepared to deal with any issues—will help to ease tensions.

thus not fully protected from various canine diseases. If you can't avoid rest stops, bring a supply of large puppy training pads or paper table cloths and confine her to these when you stop. To let her walk anywhere other dogs have walked or eliminated puts her at risk for contracting potentially deadly diseases, the worst being parvovirus.

Bring along an empty bottle to fill with water at the breeder's kennel, because sudden changes in water can upset her young digestive tract. If your drive is longer than two to three hours, contact the breeder to find out the type of food your puppy has been eating and bring some of it with you. Avoid treats and feed her only her normal food. Why? Because treats tend to be richer than dog food and may aggravate an already distressed digestive tract. That being said, chances are good your puppy will get carsick on the ride home. This is very normal, so there is no need to be overly concerned.

Locating a Veterinarian

Before you bring your puppy home, locate both a regular *and* an emergency veterinarian. Keep the phone numbers and hours for both clinics posted where they can quickly be found by any member of your family. You should also post the 24-hour, seven-day-a-week Pet Poison Helpline number (1 (800) 213-6680). You will be charged a small fee to speak with a professional, but this could save time and even your puppy's life!

Here are some suggested questions to ask a prospective veterinarian:

- How long is the wait for a non-emergency appointment?
- How available is he or she for emergencies?
- How many years has he or she been in the community?
- How many veterinarians, nurses, and technicians does the clinic have?
- Does the clinic have a specialty? Some clinics are geared toward general practice, while others specialize in surgical procedures, cats, exotics, and so forth. Make sure that dogs make up the bulk of the practice.
- Does he or she have experience in identifying and treating the common health issues of Golden Retrievers?

BE PREPARED! Be Sure That Your Budget Can Handle a Dog!

The cost of owning a dog often sneaks up on owners. The average annual outlay for a dog is over $1,500. Surprising, isn't it? Here are some average costs to consider, remembering that prices in your region may be more or less than average:

- Food, vitamins, and treats: $450
- Veterinary exams, laboratory work, and vaccinations: $225
- Heartworm, flea, and tick preventatives: $300
- Grooming: $110
- Boarding: $200
- Toys: $50
- Miscellaneous: $200

Costs will be even higher during a puppy's first year because of all the one-time gear purchases (multiple collars, crates, food bowls, and so on), training classes, and multiple veterinary visits (for vaccinations, deworming, and spay/neuter), not to mention potential adjustments to your home and property, such as a fence and baby gates.

And, if your Golden develops any of the medical issues common to the breed, expect your veterinary bills to increase significantly. A weekend trip to the emergency veterinarian is always a large pain in the wallet.

You can see how easily the costs of owning a Golden can add up. Before you commit to bringing a dog into your family, take an honest look at your budget and make sure you are in a financial position to support this new member of the family.

You also need to decide the type of veterinarian you want to use; a traditional veterinarian, a holistic veterinarian, or a veterinarian who embraces the best of both philosophies, known as a complementary veterinarian.

Your veterinarian and clinic staff are your partners in caring for your dog. Always feel free to ask them any questions or share any concerns you have regarding your Golden's health.

Schedule a preliminary examination with your veterinarian for your new puppy before you pick her up from the breeder. You will also need to schedule follow-up visits to complete her vaccinations.

CAUTION

Until your puppy is fully vaccinated at 16 weeks, keep her in your lap or a travel kennel and avoid letting her walk on the floor anywhere in the veterinary clinic. Without her full set of vaccinations, your puppy is vulnerable to disease and needs to be protected.

SHOPPING LIST

Puppy Gear

As your puppy grows, you will need to purchase increasingly larger gear for her. Collars and harnesses are of particular importance, but they are not the only items you will need to purchase in larger sizes as she grows. Don't be surprised if you become a regular visitor to the pet supply store during her first year. Your puppy will grow fast, and you need her gear to keep pace with her growth!

Here is a list of puppy gear you will need to purchase before you bring home your new Golden puppy.

✔ Crate
✔ Collar
✔ Harness
✔ Two leashes: one 6 foot (2 m) leash and a 15–50-foot (5–15 m) check cord.
✔ Identification tags (use both your cellular and home phone numbers)
✔ Food and water bowls
✔ Puppy food
✔ Training treats
✔ Several sturdy, size- and age-appropriate toys
✔ Slicker brush
✔ Pin brush
✔ Comb
✔ Puppy shampoo and conditioner
✔ Baby gates

FYI: Give Your Golden a Great Head Start

Check out the AKC's new S.T.A.R Program at *www.akc.org/starpuppy*. This program, perfect for new and experienced dog owners, is designed to get owners and puppies off to a good start in four primary areas: socialization, training, activity, and responsibility. It will answer many of your puppy-raising questions and is an excellent preliminary program as you work toward your Golden's CGC (Canine Good Citizen) certification.

The First Wellness Visit

Schedule a new puppy wellness visit with your veterinarian for within the first two days of bringing her home. Bring along the vaccination and deworming diary you received from your breeder. This will help your veterinarian determine which vaccines your pup needs and when it's best to have her vaccinated. The veterinarian will also want a stool sample, so be prepared.

Crates and Crate Training

Types of Crates: Plastic Versus Wire

There are two primary types of crates, the hard plastic style and the wire style. Which one you choose depends on your preferences and lifestyle.

Hard plastic crates with "windows" for airflow come in a variety of sizes and provide an enclosed, den-like environment. A wire crate is more open and also comes in an assortment of sizes. Both crates are safe, functional choices for your puppy. Whichever crate style you choose, the door should have two latches, one on the top and one on the bottom. A single latch in the center can be dangerous because a dog desperate to get out of a crate can force her head into the upper or lower area, get stuck, cut her airflow, and die. The metal of the crate must be high quality, as weak metal can bend easily and injure your Golden or enable her to escape. An additional benefit of wire crates is that some offer two door options—one door on the side and another on the end—which gives you more flexibility in placing and positioning the crate. If you choose a wire crate, cover the outside with a sheet, blanket, or kennel cover to create a den-like space. If you plan to travel with your Golden, be aware that airlines require the hard plastic style and do not accept pets in wire crates. Also, hard plastic crates tend to be the crates of choice for hunters, especially if traveling with multiple dogs.

Crate Comfort

Start with a small crate with just enough room for your puppy to stand up and turn around, or block off a section of a larger crate. You want your puppy to have only enough room to lie down comfortably; otherwise your pup will do her business in one end of the crate and sleep in the other.

Call me paranoid, but I am not a fan of putting bedding in a crate with a puppy or dog who has a history of chewing things. Puppyhood is a time of intense chewing, and, trust me, your Golden is going to do a lot of it! It is far too easy for an unattended Golden to not only chew up a bed, but also to ingest it. And don't count on beds advertised as chew-resistant to actually be chew-proof. It's a nice marketing device, but my mouthy Golden has chewed through one of the top-rated chew-resistant beds—several times! This can have tragic consequences (see Intestinal Blockages on page 92). Until you are confident your Golden will not chew her bedding, I would recommend nothing but a sturdy, chew-proof toy to go in the crate with her.

Crate training promotes positive discipline and creates a routine for your puppy. Teach your Golden (no matter what age) that the crate is the best thing in the world. Make sure every interaction she has with her new den is pleasant.

How to Crate Train

I strongly advise against placing the crate in the basement or some out-of-the-way place. Make it a part of the family environment, and, if possible, place the crate near you when you are home. Remember, your Golden is at her most content when she is near you, and this encourages her to go into it without feeling lonely or isolated. A good location for the crate is a central room in the home, such as the living room or kitchen, or the entrance to a large hallway. You may want to consider having more than one crate. Put one in the kitchen for daytime use and another in the bedroom for nighttime use. Wherever you put her crate, give your new puppy a few days to get used to her new den, and praise her every time she goes near it.

After family introductions, guide your Golden to her crate and have some treats or a favorite toy tucked inside for her. Close the door with your puppy outside her crate; your goal is to get her so interested in getting inside that she paws and begs you to open the door. Now open the door, let her enter the crate to get her reward, and praise her with words such as *"Good puppy"* (see "FYI: That's My Name, Don't Wear It Out!" on page 119 for information on why you don't want to use her name too frequently) and lots of loving pats. Then, let her out and ignore her. You want too downplay the exit, so that she doesn't interpret being outside of the crate as better than

FYI: Benefits of Crate Training

- It provides a safe place where your Golden can be away from others.
- It provides a place for good, solid rest. Uncrated dogs tend to be on guard duty.
- It facilitates housetraining, because dogs are naturally reluctant to soil the space where they sleep.
- It makes for a comfortable bed and sleeping environment. It also prevents her from roaming the house at night.
- It serves as a temporary playpen when you are unable to monitor her.

being inside. If she doesn't enter the crate right away, do not try to force her. At this early stage, use only inductive methods. (The exception to this is overnight crating. You may need to place her in her crate and shut the door upon retiring. If the crate is next to your bed, you can easily reach over and offer a reassuring word or a quick pat through the wire.)

Repeat this exercise several times, each time increasing the amount of time she is in the crate with the door shut. She may start whining, barking, or scratching the door, and if this is the case, make her next confinement shorter. Again, you want this to be a positive experience. When she has this routine down, start saying the word "*Crate*" or "*Kennel*" as she enters the crate.

After introducing your Golden puppy to the crate, begin feeding her regular meals in it in order to reinforce the pleasant association. If she readily enters, put the food dish in the back of the crate, but if she is still reluctant to go inside, put the dish only as far inside as she will voluntarily go without becoming fearful or anxious. Each time you feed her, position the dish a little further back in the crate. Once she is standing comfortably in the crate to eat her meal, you can close the door. When you begin this training, open the door as soon as she finishes her meal. With each subsequent feeding, leave the door closed a few minutes longer until she stays in the crate for 10 to 15 minutes after eating.

Spend the next couple of days practicing these exercises, and, while your puppy is in the crate, practice going in and out of the room, checking in every few minutes to get her accustomed to you coming and going.

When you let her out of the crate, quietly and calmly open the door and direct her outside to the designated potty area. If her crate is not close to the exit door, pick her up and carry her outside; if you let her walk, and there is any kind of distance to the door, there's a good chance she will eliminate on the floor. Repeat this process a few times before you leave for longer periods of time, and always make sure your puppy empties her bladder before you go. You may want to consider leaving a radio playing as this creates a comfortable and familiar atmosphere for your puppy. Start slowly and build up to longer periods of time away from your puppy.

HOME BASICS
Crate Rules

The crate serves as a wonderful training tool; however, there are some rules to keep in mind.

- The crate should never be used for punishment. Brief time-outs are okay, but you must control your temper so that your puppy does not develop negative associations with her crate.
- Be careful not to overuse the crate. This is not where your Golden should live. If crate time is excessive, she may not have enough time for exercise and social interaction with family members, both of which are critical to her development. By crating her too much, you will create other problems, such as fearfulness of people and new things. It may also cause aggressive behaviors.
- Never force your Golden into her crate, as this creates fear and resentment. Tossing in a treat is a much easier way to get her in the crate.

Do not use the crate when:

- Your puppy is too young to have sufficient bladder or sphincter control for the duration of the confinement.
- Your puppy has diarrhea.
- Your puppy is vomiting.
- Your puppy has not eliminated shortly before being placed inside the crate.
- Your puppy has not had sufficient exercise, companionship, and socialization.

Do not leave a bowl of food or water inside the crate while the puppy is unattended, because eating and drinking causes the need to eliminate. That being said, if your puppy is to be confined for more than two hours, you may want to add a small hamster-type water dispenser for her.

The crate's placement in a temperature-controlled environment is also important, because you don't want your puppy to get too hot or too cold.

Separation Anxiety If your puppy has separation anxiety, confinement may escalate the problem. Behaviors resulting from separation anxiety include:

- Continuous barking for 30 minutes or longer
- Urination or defecation in the crate
- Damage to the crate
- Moving of the crate
- Wet chest fur and saliva on the floor from drooling
- Consistent destructive behavior when she is left alone
- Following you from room to room
- Frantic greetings upon your return

Here are some things you can do at home to ease your puppy's separation anxiety:

- Keep your comings and goings low key. Don't chat up the puppy before you leave ("Oh, poor baby! Mommy/Daddy is sooo sorry to leave you!") and simply ignore her for at least 15–20 minutes after you return. Remember, she is a dog, not a human, and the pack leader coming and going without so much as a glance in her direction is perfectly normal.
- Take your Golden for a good, solid run or walk before leaving her, so any pent-up stress is dissipated before she is left alone.
- Watch to see if she is picking up cues to your departure—for example, picking up your keys. If so, desensitize her to this by picking up your keys repeatedly and frequently without leaving.
- Leave a radio turned on so she isn't in a completely silent house.
- Develop a leaving routine. A frozen toy, stuffed with some of her food and some extra yummy things, is an excellent treat and keeps her busy so she doesn't react to being left alone. She may even get to the point of looking forward to your leaving!
- Think about taking her to a doggy daycare a few days a week so she can socialize, play, and exhaust herself. This will release a lot of stress and make her more apt to sleep the next day when she is left alone.

If your puppy has excessive separation anxiety problems that you cannot fix yourself, talk to a professional trainer about solutions.

Important Crate Tips
- Always remove your puppy's collar before putting her in the crate, as it can get caught on the bars or mesh wire. If you must keep the collar on for identification purposes, use a break-away safety collar.
- If your puppy messes in her crate while you are out, do not punish her when you return. Simply wash out the crate using a pet odor neutralizer.
- Do not allow children to play in your Golden's crate or to handle her while she is in the crate. The crate is her private getaway, and everyone should respect her space.

Housetraining Your Golden Puppy

Vigilant is a good description of the state you should be in when housetraining a puppy. Puppies need to eliminate after playing, eating, drinking, waking up, and anytime in between.

There She Goes Again!
Accidents happen! They're just part of owning a puppy. As a new Golden Retriever owner, you will quickly learn that your first priority is housetraining. Patience and vigilance are required during this process. Every puppy is different, and it can take a few weeks or several months for a puppy to be fully housetrained.

From the first day you bring your puppy home, train her to eliminate outside of the house. Paper training a puppy and then re-training her to eliminate outside just prolongs the entire process and causes confusion. Dogs naturally develop preferences for going in certain places or on distinct surfaces like grass; however, if you don't proactively train her to go outside, she will choose a convenient place inside your home. The keys with house-training are consistency and reward.

It is very important to know how often your puppy eliminates. If she eats, drinks, or plays excessively, she naturally will need to go more often. Since puppies can't hold it for a lengthy period of time, you must give her plenty of opportunities to eliminate. One way to help you predict her need for a bathroom break is to keep a record of your puppy's urinating and defecating for several days in a row. Start by determining the minimum interval between elimination, subtract 15 to 20 minutes from that, and you have your puppy's temporary "safety zone." This is the duration of time she can generally be trusted to hold her urine after eliminating (provided she doesn't drink a lot of water during this time). However, make sure you closely supervise her any time she is not confined to her crate. If you see her beginning to circle or squat, scoop her up immediately and take her outside to the designated elimination area.

How Long Can My Puppy Hold It?

How long a puppy can comfortably hold her bladder depends on her size and age. Generally speaking, at two months, a puppy should be able to hold it for two hours; at four months, four hours; at six months, six hours; and at seven months, most puppies are able to hold their bladders for eight hours. Now, if your four-month-old

HOME BASICS
How to Prevent Accidents

Here are some of proactive steps that you can take to help prevent your puppy from eliminating inside.

Close Off Inappropriate Areas
Whenever possible, keep your puppy away from risky areas or surfaces, such as rugs and carpeting. If your puppy suddenly runs out of the room, she may be looking for a secret spot to eliminate, so close doors to rooms where she may be tempted to do her business.

Supervise, Supervise, Supervise
Supervise your puppy by keeping her on a leash, using gates, closing doors, and so on. Be alert. If she has frequent accidents in the house, she may develop a preference for those locations, which will make it harder for her to learn to eliminate outside. Every time your puppy eliminates in the house it reinforces a habit—a bad habit. In short, she must be supervised at all times. If you cannot supervise her, put her in her crate with a sturdy chew toy.

Catch Her in the Act
If you catch her in the act, say in a loud voice (no yelling!), "*Outside!*" (once is enough), and whisk her off to her elimination spot outside. Then, in your normal, neutral voice say, "*Let's go outside*" or "*Let's go potty.*" Guide or carry her to your preferred spot to let her finish. Do this even if it appears she is done.

Then ask yourself what *you* missed. The puppy isn't to blame here; somewhere along the line, you made a mistake and either did not follow the schedule or missed her cues.

If you find a puddle or pile, simply clean it up. Use a cleanser that neutralizes pet odor or, if not available, white distilled vinegar, soap, and water. Do not use ammonia-based cleansers, because they smell like urine to your Golden.

Never Use After-the-Fact Discipline
Never, *never* discipline your Golden (verbally or otherwise) for house soiling accidents you did not witness. She will have no idea why you are angry, and discipline will only serve to confuse her. Again, you are more to blame than she is.

Never Punish Submissive Urination
When a puppy is overly excited or feeling submissive, she can involuntarily urinate. Typical triggers of submissive urination are eye contact, verbal scolding, hovering over, reaching out to pet her head, animated movements, talking in an excited or loud voice, and strangers or visitors approaching. Don't punish your puppy for this behavior or the problem could get worse. Don't worry; she will likely grow out of it. If the submissive urination is frequent or has not stopped entirely by the time she reaches her first birthday, consult your veterinarian.

puppy can't go more than two hours without an accident, then work within her schedule and provide timely potty breaks. (If your puppy is urinating very frequently, this may indicate a urinary tract infection and the need to contact the veterinarian.)

Consistency Is Key

Within the first couple of days that your new Golden puppy is home with you, try to develop a sleeping, eating, playing and napping routine in order to establish patterns for her. For example, you know your pup should always go outside when she first wakes up and before she retires to her crate. She should also go outside within 30 minutes after eating, so scheduling meals at the same time every day helps you to know when to take her outside.

When you are about to take your puppy outside, say a trigger phrase such as *"Do you want to go outside?."* *"Do you want to go potty?"* or *"Hurry up!"* Say this phrase *every* time you take her out to help her make the association, and say it with excitement and a happy look on your face—even if it's 5:00 A.M.!

When taking your puppy outside the first few times, it is important that you stay with her until she has done her business, because not all puppies completely empty their bowels or bladder on the first go. You may need to stay out a bit longer until your puppy has her second or third elimination; you will get to know her habits fairly quickly.

When a puppy goes outside, she wants to do everything *but* her business. With so many smells and interesting things to explore, your Golden will be easily distracted, so make sure she associates outside with doing her business rather than play. To help this along, continually say trigger phrases such as *"Go outside,"* *"Go potty,"* *"Hurry up,"* and so on. If this doesn't do the trick, try putting her on a leash and taking her to the designated elimination area every time you take her outside. This way, *you* control where she goes.

Praise and Reward

When your Golden eliminates, praise her in your regular tone of voice. Although you may feel like jumping for joy and loudly expressing how happy you are, don't, as it could startle her. Simply praise her and reward her with a treat the very instant she is done eliminating. Timing is critical. If you delay the praise and treat, she may think you are rewarding her for walking to the house, and not for eliminating outside. Praise and reward her every time she eliminates until she is fully housetrained.

Housetraining Problems

If you find that you have a difficult time housetraining your puppy, ask yourself the following questions:

- *Did I leave her alone too long?* If the answer is yes, take her outside more frequently.

- *Is the crate or room too big?* If the answer is yes, block off part of the extra space.
- *Is she drinking too much water out of boredom or habit?* If the answer is yes, consider giving her less water and involve her in activities to break the boredom.
- *Does she have a urinary tract problem or other medical condition?* If the answer is yes or maybe, talk to your veterinarian.

Housetraining Signals

Using a bell and speaking are two very effective methods to help your Golden let you know when she needs to go outside.

Bell Method At the door you use to take your puppy in and out for elimination, hang a small bell at the height of the puppy's nose. (Remember, it will have to be moved upward as she grows.) Each time you go outside with her, physically take her nose or paw, ring the bell, and then open the door. Your puppy will soon correlate the two and run to the door to ring the bell herself.

Speaking Method Another valuable tool to use, once your puppy is housetrained, is teaching her to speak on command. When you are at the door, say, *"Do you want to go outside? Speak!"* When she speaks, praise her, open the door, and take her outside. Use the same exercise to go back inside the house. This is a great command for your puppy to learn, because it can be used anywhere, at any door.

Preventing Biting and Mouthing

Biting and mouthing are normal social activities for young puppies when playing with their littermates, and your Golden puppy will naturally extend this behavior to her new pack members—you and your family. Unlike adult canine teeth, puppy teeth are needle fine and extremely sharp. It is important to teach your puppy what is and is not appropriate when it comes to using her sharp teeth.

The first order of business when training your Golden puppy is to control her biting reflex. This is called bite inhibition. Your Golden puppy would normally learn bite inhibition from her mother and littermates. However, since puppies are taken away from their mothers at a young age, it is up to her human family to teach her not to bite.

One great way to inhibit the biting reflex is to allow your puppy to play and socialize with other puppies and well-socialized older dogs. If your puppy becomes too rough while playing, the other puppy will give a very loud, sharp cry. It's through this type of socialization that your puppy learns to control her biting reflex.

Breed Truths

Use Her Natural Instincts to Teach Bite Inhibition

All puppies bite and nip, but Goldens' are one of the easiest breeds to teach not to do this. You can actually use your puppy's mouthiness to your advantage in training her to not bite. If your puppy wants attention from you, put a toy in her mouth before you begin to pet her. If she drops the toy, the petting stops. If she does bite, quickly put the toy in her mouth. If she drops the toy and bites again, gently give her a time-out in her crate. By denying her your attention and company, you are punishing her in a way that she can understand and also playing upon another instinctual desire of hers, which is to be close to you.

Feeding Puppies

The Association of American Feed Control Officials (AAFCO) makes a nutritional distinction between adult dog food and puppy food, which is higher in protein, fat, calcium, phosphorus, and sodium. Contrary to popular thinking, a fat puppy isn't necessarily a healthy puppy. It's important to manage your Golden's growth in order to promote healthy bone and joint development. Research suggests that keeping your Golden slim and trim throughout her life may decrease her risk of developing cancer, and rapid growth has also been linked to greater incidences and severity of orthopedic issues, such as hip and elbow dysplasia. Ask your breeder if his or her puppies are on a "slow-grow plan" and what you need to do to continue the program. If they're not, work with your veterinarian to manage your puppy's diet and

FYI: The Slow-Grown Plan

A study done on Labrador Retriever puppies fed a restricted diet and kept trim throughout their lives showed a significantly reduced rate of cancer and delayed onset of cancer when compared to their littermates. Many in the Golden Retriever community believe a restricted diet may help reduce incidence of cancer in the breed. While there are no studies yet to support it, a diet rich in antioxidants may also have protective value.

growth. Maintaining a healthy weight from puppyhood on gives your dog a better-quality and, hopefully, a longer life.

Feeding Schedule

The following is a general guideline as to how often you should feed your dog:

- Eight weeks to four months: three feedings per day.
- Four months to twelve months: two feedings per day.
- Over twelve months: one feeding per day, either morning or night.

Young puppies sometimes throw up bile when their stomachs are empty, usually during the night or first thing in the morning. Possible solutions are to feed her closer to bedtime, increase the number of meals she gets in a day, or give her a puppy cookie just before bed. If the problem persists, call your veterinarian.

Chapter Five

Living with a Golden Retriever

Living with a Golden Retriever is so good for the ego! Goldens are bred to be intensely focused on their handler, and this constant attention to your every want and whim makes you feel on top of the world. It can also be a tad annoying when you get up to grab a glass of water and you have a shadow following you to the kitchen. But that's life with a Golden. She is programmed to be at the ready for anything you may need her to do, and if you go out of range, she needs to follow to make sure that she is— you guessed it—ready. She wants to be close to you, so get used to checking the floor before you put down the footrest on the recliner or step out of bed. Training your Golden should be a top priority for you, so be sure to read Chapter 7, where we discuss training basic house manners that will help you work with some of her inbred tendencies.

Mouthy to an Extreme!

If there is a mouthier dog breed out there, I don't know about it! Goldens are mouthy to an extreme, which makes them phenomenal hunting dogs and standout assistance dogs, but can create some interesting challenges for life in your home. As you read in the previous chapter, the good news is you can turn this mouthiness to your advantage when training your puppy—and you may never have to get your slippers again!

Mouthiness can also make coming home a bit of a laugh. Don't be surprised to walk in the door, have your Golden say a quick hello, and then disappear. Where has she gone? To find the very best of all her toys, so she can present it to you! The first time one of my dogs did this, I was afraid she wasn't feeling well, until she came back, tail plumes whipping madly, with her precious rubber frog in her mouth! Yes, I was honored. The frog was her favorite toy and she had to hunt it down especially for me. Such devotion is humbling.

While your Golden's mouthiness can be entertaining, it can also pose some serious dangers for her. You need to make your home, including your yard and garage, safe for your dog. Goldens interpret their world with their noses and mouths, so keeping potentially harmful things out of reach is critical.

Behavior Generalization

Ever wondered why your Golden sits like a pro at home and at training class, but won't sit when you go for a walk, take her to the park, or while the kids are playing video games? Or why she is perfectly housetrained at your home, but seems to always urinate in the house when you take her to your mother-in-law's? It's probably because she has not generalized the behaviors. In other words, your Golden has learned to sit in very specific circumstances, and now you need to broaden those circumstances and situations so she will understand that "*Sit*" means sit, no matter where she is and what is going on around her. And while she knows exactly which door to go to and where to eliminate outside at your house, she needs to be taught this again every time you bring her somewhere new.

Every new situation presents a fresh learning opportunity for you and your Golden, until she has mastered her training and can perform on command in any and all situations. Early behavior generalization is particularly important if you are planning to participate in sporting events or to work with your Golden. While to you there may not be much of a difference between a nursing home and a children's hospital, to your Golden it is a brand-new place, with absolutely no correlation to the nursing home she visited yesterday. It has distinctive noises, topography, and smells, and the people have a very different energy. You will need to understand this and work with her to generalize her pet therapy education by reviewing her training in this new environment. The same thing goes for hunting dogs. The field behind the hunt club is a wholly different place than an AKC field trial. A hunting Golden needs to be trained to generalize her skills to varied environments; it is best to begin this training when she's a young pup and continue it throughout her life.

CAUTION

Patience Is the Key— Control Your Temper

It is important never to hit or slap your Golden, either during training or at any other time. Physically reprimanding her won't stop her from misbehaving; it will simply scare and confuse her. Physical punishment is the surest way to erode the trust and respect that form the basis of an effective training program.

Feeding

When you look down on your Golden, she should have a waist, and when you run your hands along her sides, you should be able to feel her ribs. Obesity is a potential health hazard for any dog, and it's important that you keep her fit and trim.

Your breeder should be able to tell you your dog's potential adult height and ideal target weight. From there, I recommend you follow the Hovan Slow-Grow Plan, which has specific weight and exercise benchmarks to control growth, until she reaches maturity.

Because the quality and caloric density of dog foods vary greatly, it's not possible to tell you to feed your dog "X" amount of food per day. However, for an active dog, you can use these daily caloric guidelines.

Weight	Calories per day
55 pounds (25 kg)	1550–1800
65 pounds (30 kg)	1650–1950
75 pounds (34 kg)	1950–2250

If your Golden is working as a field dog, you need to provide her with more calories when you are actively training or in the field. It's best to feed her lightly while you are hunting, and then let her catch up on her calories when she gets back home. Here are some caloric guidelines for when she is actively working or field training.

Weight	Calories per day
55 pounds (25 kg)	1750–2200
65 pounds (30 kg)	1850–2350
75 pounds (34 kg)	2050–2450

FYI: How to Change Dog Food

If you do it too quickly, changing your Golden's food can create unpleasant and odiferous digestive issues. Changing to a new food should be done gradually over the course of three to four weeks.

- Week One: 25 percent new food, 75 percent old food.
- Week Two: 50 percent new food, 50 percent old food.
- Week Three: 75 percent new food, 25 percent old food.
- Week Four: 100 percent new food.

Your Golden's stools may soften when the new food is introduced, particularly when you move to the 50/50 mixture. If this is the case, hold steady at this point until her stools return to their normal form, and then keep feeding her the 50/50 mixture for another week. Once that week has passed with no digestive upset, move on to the 75 percent new/25 percent old mixture.

Don't rush this process because you only have half a bag of her old food left and don't want to buy more. Making this change too quickly will cause your dog distress and potentially create a nasty mess for you to clean up. Resign yourself to the possibility that you may need to buy more of the food you are trying eliminate.

Once again, it's important to know what normal is for your dog, so you will notice any changes in her weight. Sudden weight loss or gain, not attributable to a change in her diet, is a cause for concern and warrants a trip to the veterinarian.

Exercise

Exercise is critical to your Golden's development, but it must be carried out with care, particularly when she is young. In order to protect her growing bones and joints, avoid running or biking with your young Golden on hard surfaces. Controlled walking, with increasing distances as she grows, will keep her trim and provide the muscle needed to support her skeletal system. Talk to your veterinarian about how much exercise is appropriate. If it can be done in a safe environment, free walking or running is the best exercise, because it allows her to move at her own pace and allows for more lateral movements, which develop additional muscle mass and agility.

It is important to keep your Golden in good physical condition year-round. If you are participating in a seasonal sport, such as hunting, it is critical you begin conditioning her for the extra activity six to eight weeks in advance, so her stamina and lung power increase, and her foot pads toughen up. Goldens, like people, don't go from couch potato to star athlete overnight. If you don't condition her for an increase in activity, you run the risk of injuring her.

And even though your Golden may be entering her golden years, she still needs regular exercise. Keeping her muscles in good condition will support her joints, which, over the years, have probably developed some arthritis and become a bit stiff and creaky. Keeping her moving lubricates those creaky joints and prolongs her ability to enjoy your walks together. As with humans, this is a move it or lose it situation, so keep the old girl moving, even if it's at a snail's pace.

HOME BASICS
Golden-Proof Your Home, Yard, and Garage

Before you bring your Golden home, you need to make your home and property safe for her. Your Golden's instinct is to seek things out, put them in her mouth, and bring them to you, so you need to be very careful that what she finds and puts in her mouth is safe! Accidental injuries can be avoided to a large extent by following a few simple tips. Remember, Goldens are mouthy dogs, and until taught differently, they have the potential to swallow anything. Also, what passes for dog-proof changes as she grows, so until she reaches her full height, you need to continually adjust for her ever-increasing size.

- Close doors or set up baby gates to rooms that you don't want your puppy getting into.
- Get all plants, electrical cords, and curtain or shade pulls out of her range. I also advise covers for electrical sockets.
- Keep kids' toys picked up and out of reach. Ingested toys can cause bowel obstructions.
- Put remote controls and video game equipment (which often get left on the floor) in a secure location. Have I mentioned, Goldens are mouthy?
- Elevate your wastebaskets. Gross as it sounds, dogs love dirty tissues and other nasty things that are put into the trash!
- Keep a tight lid on your garbage. There may be things in your garbage that are deadly for your Golden Retriever. For example, leftover chicken bones can do a tremendous amount of damage to her digestive tract.
- Lock up your dirty laundry. You know that basket of stinky laundry? It smells like a banquet to your Golden! Sometimes they

come out the other end … and sometimes they don't. When they don't, it creates a medical emergency for your Golden and a financial crisis for your wallet.

- Check your yard products. Fertilizers, pesticides, and herbicides can be very toxic to your Golden, who is going to spend a lot of her time in the yard with her nose to the ground.
- Hide and secure all medications and chemicals. This is important in your house, your shed, and your garage. Even if you don't think your Golden will ever be in these areas, clean them up anyway. Goldens are quick, and the last thing you want is your dog slipping into the garage and lapping up antifreeze, which is almost always fatal.
- Bathrooms are a high-risk zone for puppies. With so many interesting-smelling bottles of medications, bathroom supplies, and cleaning products, your Golden's curiosity could get her into a sticky situation—or two! Keep these items up high or locked up. And keep the lid down on the toilet! You don't want your puppy drinking from the toilet or, worse, falling in head-first and drowning! Remember, she is a water dog, and the toilet can be an indoor playground for her.
- Don't forget the tail! Make sure all breakables are above tail level.
- See that your fencing is in good order and check it regularly.

Bottom line? Until she has matured, you must constantly watch your Golden. If you can't, put her in her crate out of harm's way. Anything she chews and swallows, other than her food, has the potential to make her sick or, worse, kill her.

Getting Touchy-Feely with Your Golden

Begin desensitizing your Golden puppy to being touched right away. Gently touch her feet, look between the pads, run your hands all over her body, lift her tail, lift her paws up, flip up her ears to have a peek inside, and check her teeth on both sides and in the front. This is important for two reasons. First, if she is used to being touched when she is feeling fine and at home, then it will be much easier for you, a show judge, or your veterinarian to inspect her in the future. Second, it is critical you know your Golden's body and what is normal for her. Why? Because by knowing what is normal, you can quickly identify when something is not as it should be. As you will read in Chapter 6, Goldens are very prone to cancer, and knowing your Golden's body can help in early detection. Things can change quickly, so give your Golden a good once-over every week for the course of her lifetime.

BE PREPARED! Yummy Things That Can Kill Your Golden!

Some human foods are very toxic to dogs. Chief among them are chocolate, grapes, and raisins, so it's very important that you make any children in your home *and* neighborhood aware of this fact. Here is a partial list of the more common toxic foods; your veterinarian can provide you with a complete list. Keep in mind that the toxic effects are not immediate for some of these foods.

- Chocolate. Toxins: theobromine and caffeine. Both are cardiac stimulants and diuretics.
- Grapes and raisins. Toxin: unknown. Can be toxic when consumed in large quantities (nine ounces or more) and can result in kidney failure.
- Xylitol. This common sugar substitute causes hypoglycemia (low blood sugar) in dogs, as well as acute and possibly life-threatening liver disease. A very small amount is all that is needed to produce toxic effects in your dog. After ingesting xylitol, dogs can begin to vomit and develop hypoglycemia within 30 to 60 minutes. Some dogs will experience liver failure within 12 to 24 hours after ingestion.
- Apples, plums, apricots, cherries, peaches (seeds, stems, or leaves). Toxin: cyanogenic glycosides. Cyanide poisoning can result.
- Onions, garlic, and onion or garlic powder. Toxin: thiosuilphate. Can cause hemolytic anemia, a breakdown of red blood cells that leaves your dog short of oxygen.
- Coffee grounds, coffee beans, and tea leaves. Toxin: caffeine. Cardiac stimulant and diuretic.
- Wild mushrooms. Toxins :vary depending on the mushroom. If you discover your Golden eating any mushroom you didn't pick up at the market, watch her closely. Get her to the veterinarian immediately if any symptoms of illness appear.
- Macadamia nuts. Toxin: unknown. A small quantity (as few as six) can cause an accelerated heart rate, skeletal muscle tremors, elevated body temperature, and weakness or paralysis of the hindquarters.
- Tobacco. Toxin: nicotine. Affects the nervous and digestive systems.
- Yeast dough. The dough will expand to many times its original size when it reaches the warm stomach of your Golden Retriever. This expansion, and the gas produced, can be very dangerous for your dog, even deadly. Also, the alcohol released from the fermenting yeast can be toxic for your dog.
- Alcohol. Your Golden is much smaller than you and has a much lower tolerance for alcohol. Therefore, she is much more vulnerable to its toxic effects.

Poison Control Center

If you think your puppy has been poisoned, call the ASPCA Animal Poison Control Center at (888) 426-4435. There is a consultation fee for this service.

Socialization

Early socialization with other well-socialized dogs and with people is critical for your Golden, because it helps her to become a well-balanced member of your family and the community at large. Make sure her socialization experiences are positive and controlled. While the dog park may seem like a great place to socialize a dog, it really isn't. It is a great place for already socialized dogs and their owners to enjoy each other's company. Because not all dogs at dog parks are well-socialized, I don't recommend taking your Golden Retriever to one before she is at least a year old, and even then, you need to watch all of her interactions carefully, looking for signs of stress or fear. One-on-one playtime with other well-socialized dogs is better than a mob at the dog park.

Breed Truths

Prey Drive

Unlike many other breeds, Golden Retrievers remain very close to their roots as a hunting dog which means they have a well-developed prey drive. Trust me, this is great if you actually hunt with your Golden, but it can be problematic when she is chasing your neighbor's Yorkie like it's a rabbit. Teach your Golden the *leave it* command in Chapter 7, early and often.

Your Golden also needs to know how to be social and polite in controlled settings. Believe it or not, you can actually over-socialize your Golden to the point that every time she sees another dog, she thinks it is a party, which can complicate even a simple walk. As with everything, you will need to strike a balance between play and controlled socializing. For example, if you take your Golden hunting and she thinks she is there to play with the other dogs, you will quickly become *persona non grata* among your hunting companions.

Your Golden and Your Children

Whether you are bringing home a Golden puppy from a breeder or from a rescue organization, any and all interactions between your children and your new dog must be closely supervised. If you can't supervise, the puppy should be safely in her crate. Until she is trained otherwise, a puppy will bite and nip, which may cause your child, as much as he loves her, to retaliate. Make sure your child understands that (1) the puppy needs to be trained, and (2) the puppy is fragile. If the puppy bites, teach your child to yell "*OUCH!*" very loudly, quickly stand up, and ignore the puppy. In the meantime, appease her natural instincts by putting a toy in her mouth.

Until they are taught, most children do not know how to safely play with a dog or puppy. Expecting your Golden to take anything and everything a child can dish out is too much to ask from even the most even-tempered of dogs. You want the relationship between the two of them to be mutually respectful, but neither the puppy nor the child has the emotional maturity to make that happen. For example, to a child a hug is a way to express his affection, but to the dog a hug is a very aggressive action that can put her immediately on the defensive. Does this mean that your child can never hug your Golden? No! It means that you need to supervise their interactions and watch your Golden's body language.

No matter what anyone tells you, all dogs will bite if pushed, even a sweet-tempered Golden. It is their only other defense besides fleeing. Be sure you and your children respect your Golden's personal space. This will

Beyond the price you pay for your new Golden puppy, there are a variety of other expenses associated with her arrival in your home, and it is best to budget for them in advance. First and foremost are veterinary expenses for her initial wellness visit and subsequent vaccination visits. Then, there is all the puppy gear that needs to be in place when she comes home and the replacement gear that will need to be purchased as she grows. Oh, and she will destroy more than a few toys along the way, so be prepared to replace those as well. She is also going to want to eat, every day, multiple times a day (kind of like your kids), so expect the kibble budget to increase in size as she does. She will require training, so plan on several training classes over her first year and, ideally, well into her second. Also, there are costs associated with participation in any sports or jobs that she may have.

go a long way toward her growing up to be the classic, gentle Golden whom the kids use as a pillow while they watch television.

Life with That Gorgeous Golden Coat

Beyond the need for regular brushing, the Golden Retriever's coat provides some extra housekeeping chores for her owners. First and foremost, Goldens shed—a lot! However, because their fur is longer, it doesn't weave into things like a Lab's fur might. Rather, it forms golden fur bunnies that float across the floor at the slightest breeze. This makes cleanup easier, but be sure to clean out the rotating brush on your vacuum cleaner after you vacuum. Why? Because those golden, gossamer fur bunnies will wind firmly around the working parts of your vacuum, rendering it ineffectual.

Then there is the oil from her coat, which can soil your carpet, walls and furniture. Walls? Yes, your walls. Like most dogs, your Golden will likely curl up to sleep with her back tucked against a wall. In our house, the favorite napping spots are all distinctly marked by large smudges on the wall, that have to be washed off periodically. If you have a Golden and you have wallpaper, make sure it is the washable variety. Trust me on this; once again, I learned the hard way.

It is best to put covers over your upholstered furniture if you allow your Golden up on the sofa or on chairs with you. Even if she isn't allowed up, I suggest you put something over the front face of the furniture, because, she will likely nap right up against the front of the sofa or chair. Washable slipcovers work great. Even better, get leather furniture.

Keeping your Golden well-groomed helps to mitigate some of the housekeeping issues, but it won't eliminate them. But who needs a spotless house when you have an amazing dog? Well, that's my excuse anyway.

10 Questions About Living with a Rescued Golden

1 **Q: Will my rescue Golden be fully trained? If she is, why does the rescue organization suggest that I go to a training class with her?**

A: Maybe. She may, like two of my rescues, be schooled in the basics but not have any house manners. Regardless of whether she appears to be trained or not, plan to take your new rescue Golden through several classes. This is a good idea for a couple of reasons. First, you both need to be on the same page with your command vocabulary. Second, and more important, classes give you the opportunity to bond and have fun with your new dog. They also set you up in a leadership position within the pack dynamic, which is very important for any dog.

2 **Q: The organization from which I adopted her told me that my new Golden was housetrained, but she is eliminating in the house! Why? What should I do?**

A: First, take her to the veterinarian to make sure there is no medical reason, such as a urinary tract infection, for the inappropriate eliminations. Once any medical cause has been ruled out, take an objective look at when she is eliminating. Is she simply squatting to urinate or defecate? If so, she may not know where she is supposed to go or how to tell you that she has to go.

Is her urination triggered by an event or interaction, indicating submissive urination? If so, keep a close eye on the context within which it occurs, and then determine how you are going to ease her distress in those situations.

3 **Q: Should I change my rescued Golden's name?**

A: That depends a lot on her circumstances. If you know for sure that she has come from an abusive situation, she likely has negative associations with her name, and changing it is a very good idea. Conversely, if she has been in a loving home, but the owners had to give her up for some reason, then there really isn't any reason to change her name, unless you just happen to prefer another. If your new rescue girl is a stray, then her name was given to her by someone in the rescue; since she doesn't have any long-term association with it, feel free to change it.

4 **Q: How do I go about changing her name without confusing her?**

A: Jane Nygaard, founder of RAGOM (Retrieve a Golden of Minnesota), gave me a very simple and effective method for changing your rescue Golden's name. Let's say your rescue girl's name is Petunia, and you want to change it to Sadie. Simply begin calling her Petunia Sadie, keeping the old name first so that she recognizes it and pays attention. Then eventually drop the Petunia and simply call her Sadie.

5 **Q: Our new Golden wants to sleep on the bed. Is this okay?**

A: Whether or not to allow a dog to sleep on the bed can be a complicated issue; the dog's desire to sleep with you may be related to dominant behavior, or she may merely want to sleep with the pack. If your rescue dog's background is documented and she has a habit of sleeping on the bed, then letting her do so with you can actually facilitate her transition. On the other hand, if your new girl's history is unknown, it is best to have her sleep on her own bed rather than on yours.

6 **Q: My new rescue Golden seems shy. What can I do to help her?**

A: Give her space. Sit on the floor, and when she approaches give her a kind word and a tasty treat, but avoid eye contact. Why no eye contact? In the canine world, it can be read as an aggressive act. Put her crate or bed in a room just off the main living area so she can retreat if she feels the need to. Take everything slow and quiet with your shy girl and know she may eventually get over her shyness. Or she may accept you and your family but no one else, and will always look to you to provide sanctuary for her.

7 **Q: Will my rescue Golden fit right in with our family?**

A: Given time, yes. All members of the family will need to give her time to adjust, because she isn't going to be everyone's best buddy right away. If you have children, let her approach the kids and tell them to keep their movements slow. If they want to stroke her, just a short pet on the side or under the chin is best. Patting the top of the head can be interpreted as aggressive. And no hugging—by anyone! Dogs in general don't like to be hugged, but a rescue can interpret this as a very aggressive move and react accordingly. Again, your new rescue Golden will need time to adjust to her new life and family.

8 **Q: Why is the behavior of my adult rescue Golden so different from my Golden whom I raised from a puppy?**

A: Quite simply, she has had a very different life, good or bad. She was raised by different people, with different rules, and may or may not have been treated kindly. One of my rescues thought that trash and counters were fair game when it came to food, so we had to teach him otherwise.

9 **Q: Why are the first two weeks in my home so critical to my new rescue Golden?**

A: Coming into a new home is extraordinarily stressful for your new Golden. Remember, she doesn't know or have any reason to trust you—yet. Let her explore her new world and people on her own terms. Don't have any expectations for her the first two weeks other than that she get know you and your family. Don't invite friends or relatives over; adjusting to her new home and family is enough stress for her. During the first week, she is a true flight risk, so keep her on a check cord at all times to manage her movements. Do not leave her unattended outside, even if you have a fenced yard. A frightened dog can jump over or dig under a fence.

10 **Q: Our rescue Golden has been here for a few months and her personality seems to be changing. Is this normal?**

A: Perfectly normal! And it's a good thing! It means that she is finally feeling comfortable in her new home and has adjusted to her new life.

Chapter Six

Health and Nutrition

A wareness is the starting point for optimizing the health of your Golden Retriever. A variety of factors have a direct impact on your dog's health and well-being. These include the health of her parents and extended family, the quality of her nutrition, the quality and quantity of exercise, health care, and environmental factors.

Your veterinarian will be your partner in ensuring a lifetime of good health for your Golden Retriever. Providing clear and concise information regarding your dog and her health to your veterinarian is critical, particularly in an emergency situation. Making a list of your dog's symptoms before your visit will serve to jog your memory and is a great help to the veterinarian.

Vaccinations

Vaccines are given to stimulate the immune system into producing antibodies to defend against disease. They contain either heat-killed or live pathogens treated to make them less infectious, known as modified live virus (MLV). Recently, a new class of recombinant vaccines has been developed, which uses DNA to stimulate the production of antibodies.

Active immunity occurs when a dog is exposed to an infectious disease, which stimulates her body to create antibodies against that disease and subsequently protects her from reinfection. Active immunity takes place either when she becomes ill with the disease or when she is vaccinated. Typically, a viral immunity remains active longer than a bacterial immunity; however, depending on the dog, some illness-induced immunities can last a lifetime.

CAUTION

Leptospirosis Vaccine Allergic Reaction

The leptospirosis vaccine poses a higher than normal risk of of allergic reaction. You must watch your Golden carefully for signs of an allergic reaction after any vaccination, but particularly after she has been given the leptospirosis vaccine.

Passive immunity is acquired when puppies absorb antibodies from their mother that are passed along in her colostrum during their first 24 hours, and later, in her milk. The length of time the puppies are protected by this passive immunity depends on the concentration of antibodies in the milk.

Very young puppies need to be given a series of vaccines every three to four weeks. The primary reason for vaccinating multiple times, weeks apart, is the maternal antibodies can bind with the antigens in the vaccines, rendering them useless. Multiple vaccinations ensure that, when maternal antibody levels naturally decline, the vaccine will stimulate the puppy's own immune system into producing the needed antibodies.

Vaccines are divided into two categories, core and noncore. Core vaccines should be administered to all dogs. Noncore vaccines' use is determined by need, geographic location, and lifestyle.

Vaccinations are generally given as combination vaccines, such as DHPP (for canine distemper, hepatitis, parainfluenza and parvovirus) and DHLPP (DHPP with leptospirosis vaccine added to it, although most protocols call for the leptospirosis vaccine to be given separately from the DHPP vaccine). DHPP and DHLPP are known as minimal multivalent vaccines. While they cover the basics, there are other vaccines that contain antigens for even more diseases. Your veterinarian will help you determine the best vaccination plan for your puppy.

If you have concerns about lifelong vaccination regimes, titer testing can determine your dog's level of immunity and forestall certain vaccinations. If this is of interest to you, discuss it with your veterinarian.

Even if your Golden is vaccinated, it's important for you to read the section in this chapter describing the various diseases and their symptoms. Why? Because vaccines can fail, and if they fail, your dog or puppy can develop a life-threatening illness.

Deworming

If a stool sample indicates the litter has worms, your breeder should take care of the preliminary deworming. Testing for worms, and treatment if needed, should take place at two weeks and repeated at four, six, and eight weeks of age. Puppies can pick up worms at any age, so it's important for your Golden to have periodic stool checks as recommended by your veterinarian.

FYI: Vaccination and Booster Timetable

This chart is provided only as a guideline. Your veterinarian will know what is best for your dog and your region.

Core Vaccination	Puppy—1st Dose	Booster	Adult Revaccination
Rabies	Between 3 and 6 months	One year after first vaccine	Every 1–3 years, depending on local regulations
Canine Distemper	At 6–8 weeks, then every 3–4 weeks until age 12–14	One year of age	Every 3 years or as needed
Canine Parvovirus	At 6–8 weeks, then every 3–4 weeks until age 12–14	One year of age	Every 3 years or as needed
Canine Adenovirus 2 (also prevents Canine Hepatitis)	At 6–8 weeks, then every 3–4 weeks until age 12–14	One year of age	Every 3 years or as needed
Noncore Vaccination	**Puppy—1st Dose**	**Booster**	**Adult Revaccination**
Leptospirosis	At 12 weeks, with the second dose given at 16 weeks	Annually or every 6 months in endemic regions	
Parainfluenza	At 6–8 weeks, then every 3–4 weeks until age 12–14	One year of age	Every 3 years or every 6 months in endemic regions.
Bordetella	At 6–8 weeks with the second dose given at 10–12 weeks	Annually or every 6 months in endemic regions	
Lyme Disease	At 8 weeks, with the second dose given at 12 weeks	Annually or every 6 months in endemic regions	
Canine Coronavirus	This vaccine is no longer recommended.		
Giardia	This vaccine is no longer recommended. However, if giardia is endemic to your region, you may want to discuss this with your veterinarian.		

Spay and Neuter

For the general canine population, the spay or neuter is generally done at around the age of six months; however, data gathered by the Golden Retriever Club of America indicates significant health benefits when Goldens are spayed or neutered after the age of one year. For example, males neutered before the age of one year have an 80 percent increased risk of hypothyroidism, and females a 60 percent increased risk of hypothyroidism, as compared to those neutered after the age of one.

Because sexual hormones interact with growth hormones, physical differences can occur in dogs neutered prior to sexual maturity. They may grow taller than their genetics would normally dictate and have a long-limbed, slender look that can put added stress on the joints. Also, dogs neutered prior to sexual maturity have a greater incidence of hip dysplasia and torn cruciate ligaments than dogs neutered after one year. It's not known if this is a result of hormonal changes or a direct result of their altered structure.

Unless you purchased your Golden Retriever for the purpose of showing or breeding, spaying or neutering should happen soon after sexual maturity. For females, this is after her first heat; for males, it's soon after his first birthday. This is important for several reasons. First and foremost, spaying or neutering prevents unwanted litters of puppies, either in your home or someone else's. However, there are other positive benefits for both males and females.

Neutering your male Golden eliminates the possibility of testicular tumors and greatly reduces his chances of developing prostate disease. Spaying your female Golden eliminates her heat cycle (estrus), which otherwise brings a host of problems, from bloody discharges to unwanted attention from every intact dog for miles. Spaying also has some health benefits for your female Golden. The possibility of ovarian or uterine tumors is eliminated, and her risk of developing mammary tumors is greatly reduced. Also, the risk of pyometra, a serious infection of the womb, is eliminated.

Once your Golden has been spayed or neutered, it's important you monitor her caloric intake carefully, as the procedure can reduce the metabolic rate in both males and females. Keeping your Golden lean is important to her long-term health.

CAUTION

Know the Signs of a UTI

If your dog appears to be having difficulty urinating, needs to go frequently, or is having accidents in the house after she is housetrained, she may have a urinary tract infection (UTI). You should take her—and a urine sample—to the veterinarian as soon as possible.

HOME BASICS
Things to Regularly Check

The purpose of regular checks is threefold. First, it's important to know what is normal for your Golden, so if something changes, you will recognize it. Second, because dogs are programmed to hide any weaknesses, you may not know if your puppy is sick or injured unless you're tuned into your Golden and her body. Third, regularly checking your Golden desensitizes her to being touched, making it easier for you and your veterinarian to treat her when she needs medical attention.

Ears Goldens' floppy ears can make them vulnerable to ear problems. If you notice a foul smell, it's likely a yeasty ear infection, canker, or mites. Check inside the ears, and if you see a buildup of dirt, clean them. (Also, be sure to check the ears for any debris that may have been picked up during time in the water or field.) Once the ears are clean, check the color of the skin inside. If it's red and looks inflamed, it may be an ear infection. Ear infections can also be a symptom of allergies or hypothyroidism. If you suspect that your dog has an ear infection, get her to the veterinarian as soon as possible.

Eyes Eyes should be clear and have a small to minimal amount of discharge. If you see large amounts of discharge, or if the eyes look bloodshot or cloudy, there may be a problem, and you should visit the veterinarian.

Mouth Get into the habit of looking in your puppy's mouth to check her teeth and gums. Discuss with your veterinarian whether you need to brush your puppy's teeth.

Teeth should be white without any plaque buildup, which tends to happen near the gumline. If you see plaque developing, consult your veterinarian. Gums should be a nice shade of pink. Bright red, blue, or very pale to white gums should be brought to the attention of your veterinarian immediately, as they are indicative of a potentially life-threatening situation.

When in the field, check your dog's mouth periodically to make sure nothing other than the game has been picked up.

Stools Stools should be firm, but not hard. Changes in stool can indicate many things, and it's best to bring any changes to the attention of your veterinarian.

Paws and Pads Check nails and pads frequently to make sure they are in good order. For dogs who are training or working in the field, healthy feet are essential. Checks will get your puppy used to you handling her feet, which is very important when you need to trim her nails or remove debris. Also, keep her nails and the fur between the pads trimmed (see page 144).

Skin Thoroughly check the skin every week, looking and feeling for bumps, discolorations, changes in texture, and parasites, such as ticks and fleas.

Bodily Functions

You need to become a keen observer of your Golden's bodily functions and the resulting output. Many health issues first become evident through changes in her daily input and output. Very often, when you call the veterinarian concerned about your dog, it's because you have noticed a change in the texture, frequency, or urgency of her bowel movements.

Flatulence

While we have all laughed and gagged as a dog's flatulence clears a room, it isn't normal for a dog to pass gas on a regular basis. If flatulence comes on suddenly and is accompanied by diarrhea, abdominal pain, or a loss of appetite, you should take your dog to the veterinarian.

Scooting

Contrary to popular belief, a dog who is scooting her backside on the floor or ground doesn't necessarily have worms. She could just be a little itchy, or she may have ingested something that she is having difficulty passing. Unpleasant as it may be, you can decrease your dog's distress by removing the offending object.

However, if scooting persists, her anal sacs may be impacted, so you should contact your veterinarian. Impaction occurs when the anal sacs are not completely emptied during defecation. Over time, the fluid builds up and the anal sacs become distended and tender.

CAUTION

Diarrhea

A puppy or dog with diarrhea is at risk for dehydration and should be taken to the veterinarian. There are any number of causes for diarrhea, but it's best to get your dog to the veterinarian if it persists for more than a day.

Dog Breath

Your dog's breath shouldn't be offensive. It should have a neutral odor or smell lightly of food if she has recently eaten. A puppy's breath has a slightly sweet odor. Unless your dog has eaten something ghastly, chronic bad breath is an indicator that something isn't right. Something as simple as plaque buildup on her teeth, which over time can create a host of health issues, can be solved by regular brushing (see page 143). If the bad breath persists, see your veterinarian.

Vomiting and Regurgitation

It helps your veterinarian to diagnose the problem if you understand the difference between vomiting and regurgitation. Technically, regurgitation occurs when food in the esophagus is expelled, unforced and without retching. In contrast, vomiting is the forceful emptying of the stomach preceded by retching and often drooling. By noting your Golden Retriever's physical state as she empties her stomach, you give your veterinarian significant clues as to the cause of her stomach upset.

Vomiting is typically caused by eating hard-to-digest matter, such as grass, that irritates the stomach. However, like other bodily eliminations, vomiting can indicate a bigger problem.

Occasional vomiting is nothing to get too worried about, but you should inspect the vomit to see what your dog is bringing back up. Clean up the vomit immediately and completely, as dogs being dogs will go back and try to eat it. If it's undigested food, your puppy may be eating too fast, so try feeding smaller, more frequent meals. If the vomit looks like coffee grounds, contains blood, or smells like feces, it's possible that your dog is suffering from a bowel obstruction and needs immediate medical attention.

Breed Truths

That Plumy Fur

The lovely, long, plumy Golden Retriever fur we all love can actually pose a problem in the rectal area, particularly if your Golden is older or has hip issues and can't maintain a proper squat. If fecal matter gets caught in her fur, it can create a foul-smelling, uncomfortable mat. Keeping the fur trimmed fairly short in this area will help. If you take her to the groomer, request a "sanitary trim" which will take care of this area.

Regurgitation is cause for concern, as it may indicate an obstruction in the esophagus. If your Golden is regurgitating, call your veterinarian immediately.

Projectile vomiting is a sign something is very wrong with your dog, and you should call your veterinarian immediately. The most common cause is a gastric outflow obstruction.

If your dog is vomiting up clear, frothy bile, the causes can range from gastritis to an obstruction to bloat. Again, call your veterinarian immediately! Familiarizing yourself with the symptoms of bowel obstructions and bloat (see page 82) may just save your dog's life.

Parasites

Parasites are repulsive and disturbing … and they are actively looking for your dog. Your vigilance goes a long way toward keeping your Golden parasite-free. The most common internal parasites are roundworm, hookworm, tapeworm, and heartworm. External parasites such as fleas, ticks, and ear mites, are relatively easy to get rid of, but prevention is important because they can transfer disease and other parasites to your Golden. Ongoing parasite treatment varies depending on where you live. Work with your veterinarian to create a schedule of regular testing and treatment appropriate for your region of the country.

Roundworm

Puppies are often infested with ascarids, otherwise known as roundworms. If a stool sample tests positive for roundworms, puppies need to be treated every 2 weeks until 16 weeks of age. If your puppy is coughing or gagging, it may be a sign of roundworm larvae in her lungs. Vomiting or diarrhea may be a sign of roundworms in her stomach. Check the vomit and/or stool; roundworms look like moving strands of spaghetti, sometimes as long as 7 inches (18 cm). It's advisable to have a fecal sample analyzed to identify the type of worms present. If other worms are identified, your veterinarian may prescribe a broad-spectrum dewormer.

Hookworm

Hookworms are small, thin worms ranging in length from ¼ to ½ inch (1–1.5 cm). They reside in the small intestines and live on the blood and tissue fluids of the host. Puppies usually get hookworms from their mothers. Older dogs can get them from ingesting the larvae in soil or by ingesting an animal infected with hookworms. Hookworms can also penetrate the skin (usually the pads of the feet) and infect your Golden.

Depending on the severity of the infestation, symptoms can range from bloody or tarry diarrhea to pale mucous membranes due to anemia to weight loss and weakness. However, some dogs are asymptomatic, so an annual fecal check is recommended. (Hookworms are diagnosed by stool analysis.)

Hookworms can infect humans, so if your dog is diagnosed with hookworm, it is prudent to consult your physician.

Tapeworm

In order to be infected by tapeworms, your dog must ingest a flea or louse carrying the eggs of the tapeworm or eat an infected animal. Tapeworms live in the small intestines and can vary in size from an inch to several feet long. The head of the tapeworm fastens to the wall of the intestines, and the body is composed of segments containing eggs. These segments can sometimes be seen crawling around the anus or, when dried, appear as rice grains stuck in the fur.

The only way to kill tapeworms is to destroy the head. This requires a dewormer from your veterinarian. Keeping your Golden flea-free is the best tapeworm prevention.

Humans can be infected with tapeworms by eating uncooked, contaminated meat; by ingesting eggs passed on in the fecal matter of the dog; or by accidentally swallowing an infected flea.

Heartworm

Heartworms are a mosquito-borne blood parasite that can cause severe illness and death. Heartworms live in the right atrium and right ventricle of a dog's heart, and as their population grows, they spread to other parts of the vascular system and other organs. Your Golden should have her first heartworm test between the ages of seven and nine months, and an annual test thereafter. If your Golden is a field dog, it's critical that you protect her from heartworm, because she will definitely encounter mosquitoes while hunting. Prevention requires giving her specific medication after a negative blood test result. Preventive medications come in several forms (chewable tablets, traditional pills, liquids, and injections) and varied dosing timing (daily, monthly, and every six months). Some preventives also cover other parasites, so work with your veterinarian to create a schedule of regular testing and treatment appropriate for your Golden.

Early signs of heartworm include tiring easily, an inability to tolerate exercise, and a soft, deep cough. A blood test can determine if your dog is infected, however, if the infestation is small or she is populated with only males at the time of the blood test, a false negative can result. If you have been lax in administering heartworm preventive and have reasonable cause to suspect heartworms, ask your veterinarian to do another blood test.

Once your dog has been diagnosed with heartworms, an X-ray is needed to determine the extent of the infestation. The treatment for heartworm is harsh, and complex, taking place in stages. Due to health issues, some dogs are not candidates for treatment. It's also expensive, so it's far better to give your dog a preventive every month than to put her through treatment.

Ear Mites

Ear mites live off of the skin cells inside your dog's ears and, if left untreated, can cause bacterial and fungal ear infections. How do you know if your Golden has ear mites? She'll be scratching her ears, shaking her head repeatedly, or rubbing her head against anything and everything. If you see this behavior, take a peek in her ears. If you experience a strong, unpleasant odor or see a waxy, dark buildup, take your dog to her veterinarian, who will analyze the gunk in your dog's ear and recommend an appropriate treatment plan.

Fleas

Be aware of fleas because they can spread very quickly, especially in the summer months. Worse, they can infest your home! A female flea produces about 2,000 eggs in her four-month life span. These eggs fall off your dog and hide anywhere the dog spends time—in the ground, on her bedding, and in the carpet. You will probably see the flea dirt and eggs before you see a flea, so check your dog's skin closely, especially her belly. Flea dirt and eggs often look like salt and pepper on your dog's skin. Fleas can be prevented with a monthly liquid treatment applied between the shoulders, which results in the fleas laying infertile eggs. These products kill fleas in the dog's coat and bedding, however, they can cause burning, irritation, and allergic reactions in some dogs. Young puppies need to be closely monitored after applying the product.

Treatment and prevention options vary, ranging from flea shampoos, powders, and collars to sprays, foams, and dips. If you notice your dog has fleas, consult your veterinarian to determine the best treatment and prevention plan.

Ticks

Ticks are small, bloodsucking parasites. During your dog's first visit to the veterinarian, you should talk about the types of ticks in your area and the best way to prevent the effects and diseases resulting from a tick bite. In many parts of the country, deer ticks carrying Lyme disease strike dogs and their owners. Tick-borne diseases can be very serious, so tick prevention is critical. Products recommended by your veterinarian, including liquids applied on the back of the neck above the middle of the shoulders, will kill ticks within 24 hours. It's essential that the tick be removed or killed within 36–48 hours, before it can release the disease-causing bacteria into the bloodstream.

If you find a tick, *don't crush it*! This can transmit disease. Instead, drop the tick in a jar of rubbing alcohol to kill it. Dropping it in water won't drown it, and flushing the tick down the toilet may get it out of your house, but it won't kill it.

FYI: Lyme Disease

If you find an embedded tick, remove it as soon as possible. Lyme disease is now considered the most common tick-borne disease in the United States. Fortunately, a vaccine is now available. Signs of Lyme disease include lameness caused by the swelling of one or several joints, fever, weakness, loss of appetite, lethargy, and weight loss. A course of antibiotics given for two to four weeks is the recommended treatment.

How to Remove a Tick

Prevention is the best defense when it comes to ticks. Consult your veterinarian regarding the best prevention methods for your region and dog. Check your dog immediately after she is in an area where she could pick up ticks. The best way to check for ticks is by running your hands all over your dog, paying particular attention to the head, lips, ears, neck, and feet. Be sure to check along the edges of your dog's lips and ears, including inside the small indentation on the lower edge of the ear flap. Be sure to check inside the ear as well, as ticks will crawl into the ear canal. If the tick is in the ear canal, have your veterinarian remove it. Most dogs enjoy being checked for ticks because it feels like they are getting special attention and a bit of a massage!

If you find an embedded tick, remove it as soon as possible. Before you begin, you will need a few items:

- Rubber or latex gloves (to protect your hands from disease)
- Fine-tipped tweezers
- A small jar of rubbing alcohol
- Antiseptic
- Triple antibiotic ointment

Anatomically, the head is the weakest part of the tick, and you want to avoid it snapping off and remaining under the skin. Contrary to popular myth, applying oil or Vaseline to ticks does not cause them to back out of the skin. It does suffocate ticks and, in the process, causes them to regurgitate and deposit more disease-carrying saliva into your dog. Touching the tick with a match or lit cigarette has the same effect.

There are three methods you can employ to remove ticks.

1. Once you have located the tick and protected your hands, simply rub the tick in a fast, circular motion, maintaining your direction. After about a minute, the tick should back out of the skin. Pick it up and drop it in the jar of rubbing alcohol. This method may not work every time, but it is worth a shot, particularly if you do not have tick-removal tools close at hand. Making the tick back out of its own accord will also be less painful and stressful for your Golden.

2. If the first method does not work, grab the tick with the tweezers as close to the skin as possible, right where the mouth and head enter the skin. Do not grasp the tick by the body, as you may break the exoskeleton and release the harmful contents. Pull out the tick very gently, slowly, and steadily. Be patient. Eventually, the tick will tire and loosen its grip.
3. There are various tick-removal tools on the market. If you prefer to use one of these, ask your veterinary clinic for a recommendation.

Again, never crush a tick, as this can transmit disease. Once the tick has been removed, use an antiseptic to clean the wound left by the tick, then apply a little triple antibiotic ointment. A scab will form and the wound site may be slightly inflamed due to the irritation caused by the tick's bite. If, after a week, it is still inflamed, there may be an infection, and I suggest that you contact your veterinarian.

Diseases and Medical Conditions

The diseases and medical conditions that can affect your Golden Retriever stem from sources as varied as her physical structure (as in the case of GDV), contagious diseases, genetics, and the hazards of daily living. Recognizing the most common symptoms can ease your dog's discomfort, prolong her life, or even save it.

Bloat (GDV)

Gastric dilatation-volvulus (GDV) is the life-threatening emergency commonly known as bloat. Bloat can happen to any dog, but typically it occurs in middle-aged to older dogs. The mortality rate for bloat is high, with survival hinging on early recognition and treatment.

Contagious Diseases

Prevention is the best cure for a contagious disease. In this next section, we will look at some of the most common contagious diseases, how to avoid them, and, if avoidance fails, how to recognize the symptoms.

Parvovirus Your Golden is most vulnerable to communicable diseases such as parvovirus during her early months, before she's completely vaccinated. Parvovirus is often deadly, so it's imperative you do everything possible to keep your puppy safe. While it can affect dogs of all ages, most cases of parvovirus strike puppies between 6 and 20 weeks of age.

You can help keep your puppy healthy with these simple preventative steps:

- Keep her in a carrier or on your lap while visiting the veterinarian.
- Until she is fully vaccinated, don't take her to pet supply stores.
- Begin training at home, and then enroll in a class once she is fully vaccinated. When she does begin classes, only use training facilities that require proof of vaccination for all pet participants.

BE PREPARED! Symptoms of Bloat (GDV)

Symptoms of GDV include:

- A distended abdomen. When thumped with a finger, it sounds like a tight, air-filled drum. In the early stages, the abdomen may not be distended but may feel somewhat tight.
- Pacing and restlessness. The dog may not look distressed.
- Intense abdominal discomfort (possibly seen initially as a very "preoccupied" look on the dog's face).
- Whining or groaning when the abdomen is pressed.
- Non-productive retching or vomiting.
- Intense drooling caused by the dog's inability to swallow her saliva.
- Pale gums and tongue.
- Rapid development of severe weakness and shock.

- Keep her away from areas where other dogs have relieved themselves.
- Make sure she only socializes with other dogs and puppies who are fully vaccinated and healthy.
- Have visitors to your home leave their shoes outside. You don't know where those shoes have been, or what diseases they may be bringing in.

Symptoms of parvovirus include vomiting, depression, and sometimes a high fever up to 106°F (41°C). Diarrhea is abundant, containing blood, mucus or both. Puppies can rapidly dehydrate and will also experience intense abdominal pain, causing them to tuck up their bellies. If your puppy suddenly begins to vomit or has sudden diarrhea, get her to the veterinarian immediately.

Parvovirus requires intensive veterinary care and usually hospitalization. Fluids and medications are given intravenously in an effort to rehydrate and correct the dog's electrolyte imbalance.

Distemper Distemper is caused by a virus very similar to the one that causes measles in humans. Distemper is highly contagious and is one of the leading causes of infectious disease deaths in dogs worldwide. Vaccination is the best preventive measure. The same precautions noted for parvovirus should be taken until your Golden has had all of her vaccinations.

The distemper virus attacks brain cells and the cells lining surfaces of the body, including the skin, the membranes of the respiratory system, and the gastrointestinal tract. The first stages of the disease are characterized by a fever of 103°F to 105°F (39–41°C) accompanied by listlessness and a loss of appetite. Along with these symptoms is a watery discharge from the eyes and nose, which can cause distemper to be mistaken for a cold in the early stages. The discharge becomes thick, sticky, and yellow within a few days and is accompanied by a very noticeable dry cough. Vomiting and diarrhea

can also be present, increasing the risk of dehydration. In advanced cases, the brain is infected, causing muscle spasms and seizures.

Distemper requires veterinary treatment, and the sooner you get your dog to the veterinarian the better the prospects are for her recovery.

Kennel Cough Kennel cough is a broad term used to describe a group of highly contagious respiratory diseases. If your Golden will be around other dogs, it's a good idea to discuss vaccinating her with your veterinarian. Most kennels and many obedience classes require dogs to be vaccinated for kennel cough before accepting them as boarders or class participants.

Kennel cough is characterized by a dry, harsh cough that may persist for several weeks. If it is allowed to continue for an extended period of time, secondary bacterial infections may set in.

Kennel cough requires antibiotics. At home, isolate your dog from other dogs and keep her in a warm, well-ventilated room. A cool mist humidifier will help her to breathe easier. She will also need moderate exercise to aid in the drainage of her bronchial passages. Your veterinarian may also recommend a canine-safe cough suppressant.

Leptospirosis Leptospirosis is a bacterial infection spread by animal urine that makes its way into water sources. The bacteria enters your dog when she drinks contaminated water. It also can remain actively infectious in soil for up to six months. If your dog has any cuts or scrapes on her skin and swims in contaminated water, the bacteria can enter her system through the skin.

You should have a candid talk with your veterinarian about your Golden's lifestyle and the prevalence of leptospirosis in your region. If you choose to vaccinate your dog against leptospirosis, make sure that the vaccine covers multiple strains of the bacteria, because there is no cross-protection among the different strains.

Symptoms of leptospirosis begin with a fever, and then, over the course of a few days, depression, loss of appetite, and stiffness due to muscle pain. Blood in the urine and diarrhea may also be present. In severe cases, the eyes may appear yellow (jaundiced). Because of coagulation problems, blood may appear in the mouth and stools. These symptoms are all important to recognize, because leptospirosis infection can cause severe kidney and liver damage.

If untreated, dogs become carriers of the disease; their urine remains contaminated with the bacteria for up to a year, even if they show no signs of infection. Leptospirosis can also spread to humans. If tests confirm leptospirosis, your dog should be placed on a course of antibiotics.

Giardia Giardia is a disease caused by the *Giardia* species of protozoan and is contracted by drinking contaminated water. If you are hunting with your Golden, make sure to bring fresh drinking water from home with you. If she is retrieving waterfowl, discourage her from drinking the water, although she may ingest some while retrieving the game.

Infected adult dogs are less likely to show symptoms than young dogs, with the primary symptom being diarrhea—lots of diarrhea! It's uncharacteristically foul smelling and watery.

Giardia is diagnosed using a fecal exam. However, because the giardia oocysts are shed intermittently, three negative fecal tests, spaced two days apart are necessary, before giardia can be ruled out. Drugs are available to treat Giardia, and a vaccine is also available, but it is not often recommended because giardia is easy to treat. If your Golden's lifestyle frequently finds her in locations where she may come into contact with the giardia protozoan, you should discuss the pros and cons of vaccinating her with your veterinarian.

Inherited Diseases and Cancer

Genetics play a very important role in your Golden's health. Understanding the genetic diseases that impact the breed can help you to identify them and seek early treatment.

Approximately 60 percent of all Golden Retrievers will die from cancer. This is nearly double the one-in-three average for dogs in general. Unfortunately, cancer is endemic to the breed and affects all breeding lines, both American and English. The two most common cancers found in Golden Retrievers are hemangiosarcoma (HSA) and lymphoma.

FYI: Golden Retriever Cancer Research

How can you help with ongoing cancer research? The Canine Health Information Center (CHIC) maintains a DNA bank, and all Golden owners are encouraged to submit a DNA sample, keep the bank updated on their Golden's health throughout her life, and, when the time comes, inform the bank of the cause of death. Owners may also participate in cancer research by contacting the research facilitator of the Golden Retriever Club of America at *www.grca.org* immediately after their dog is diagnosed (prior to beginning treatment, if possible). And contributions to support Golden Retriever cancer research can be made to the Golden Retriever Foundation's Zeke Fund at *www.goldenretriever-foundation.org*.

Hemangiosarcoma (HSA) A cancer of the endothelial cells that line the blood vessels, HSA can arise in just about any tissue. The average age of death from HSA is 10.3 years. There are two forms of HSA. Cutaneous hemangiosarcoma affects the skin and underlying tissues and is often first noticed as a lump under the skin or a dark, raised rash.

The second form of HSA is visceral hemangiosarcoma, which affects the deep tissue and organs. The spleen is the most common site for tumors. Tumors of the internal organs can rupture and cause bleeding into the abdomen or, in the case of a cardiac tumor, into the pericardium (the sac around the heart). These ruptures can cause your Golden to be "off" for a few days, with a lack of appetite, lethargy, pale gums, and general weakness. She may also experience labored breathing. Once the rupture has healed, your Golden will seem back to normal. If your older Golden doesn't seem herself, I urge you to get her to the veterinarian. Unfortunately, the first sign of visceral hemangiosarcoma is sometimes sudden collapse and death.

The overall prognosis for a dog diagnosed with visceral hemangiosarcoma is limited while cutaneous hemangiosarcoma has a better prognosis. If your Golden is diagnosed with HSA, have a heartfelt discussion with your veterinarian about treatment options and their impact on your Golden's quality of life. If available, a board-certified canine oncologist may be able to offer a broader range of treatment options than your veterinarian.

Lymphoma Lymphoma (also called lymphosarcoma) is a cancer that begins in the lymph nodes and organs that contain lymphoid tissue, such as the spleen, bone marrow, and liver. The average age at which lymphoma strikes is approximately eight years. It's most often detected by feeling an enlarged lymph node, typically in the neck, armpit, groin, chest, or behind the knee. Lymphoma is a fast-spreading cancer, so if you find an enlarged lymph node, take your Golden to the veterinarian as soon as possible. The survival rate for untreated lymphoma is only 27 days, but, with treatment, most dogs can achieve a period of remission with good quality of life. The veterinarian can do a simple surgical procedure to analyze the makeup of the enlarged node. Further testing will be needed to determine how widespread the cancer is. Once a diagnosis is reached, talk to your veterinarian about possible treatment plans.

Hypothyroidism Hypothyroidism is an inherited disease and results when the thyroid doesn't produce enough of the hormones thyroxine (T4) and triiodothyronine (T3), which control the metabolic rate. It often develops in middle-aged dogs.

The most common signs of hypothyroidism are:

- Excessive shedding
- Hair loss, particularly on the front of the neck and chest, the sides of the body, and the top of the tail. Hair is dry, brittle, and falls out easily.
- Skin exposed by hair loss is thick, dry, puffy, and darker.
- Weight gain
- Weakness
- Lethargy or mental dullness
- An intolerance for cold

If you notice any of these symptoms, have your veterinarian do a simple blood test to check your Golden's hormone levels. Fortunately, hypothyroidism is easy to treat with a daily dose of a synthetic hormone called levothyroxine. This replacement hormone therapy will need to continue for the rest of the dog's life.

Atopic Dermatitis (Atopy) Your Golden is particularly susceptible to allergens inhaled or absorbed through the skin. Goldens have a genetic predisposition toward atopic dermatitis, also know as canine atopy. This is a lifelong condition that begins to show itself between the ages of one and three years.

It all begins when allergens, such as fleas, pollen, dust mite droppings, house dust, mold, human dander, and any number of other irritants, are inhaled or settle on the skin. This provokes an immune response, resulting in inflammation and itchiness. Because they are very sensitive, the ears are often the first area affected, and you may see your Golden scratching and rubbing them. Watery eyes, sneezing, and a runny nose often accompany active licking of the legs, resulting in lick granulomas (open sores), and scratching of the underside. As the scratch and itch cycle continues, sores can develop, leading to bacterial and fungal infections.

A variety of treatments can alleviate the symptoms, but, unfortunately, the affliction lasts a lifetime. Often the first recommendation is to switch your dog to a hypoallergenic diet. If that fails, further analysis is required to determine the exact cause of the allergic reaction.

The best way to avoid atopic dermatitis is to avoid the allergens, but, that isn't always possible. Medications and supplements can ease your Golden's discomfort; if she doesn't respond well to those, immunotherapy with hypersensitization (allergy shots) is available. If your Golden develops atopic dermatitis, it may be worthwhile to get a referral to a veterinary dermatologist.

FYI: Hip Certification

Currently, the only way to detect HD is with an X-ray. The following organizations are the most commonly used to read and certify X-rays.

OFA: *Orthopedic Foundation for Animals (USA).* Preliminary screening can be done at four months of age, but official certification is achieved when the dog is X-rayed at two years of age.

PennHIP: *University of Pennsylvania Hip Improvement Project.* The earliest a dog can get a PennHIP screening is four months of age, but Goldens should be screened as adult dogs for the most accurate evaluations.

Hip Dysplasia

Hip dysplasia (HD) is a structural abnormality of the hips that causes the ball at the top of the thigh bone (the femoral head) to wear against, rather than slide within, the socket (the acetabulum) in the pelvis. This wear creates painful osteoarthritis in the hip joints. Surgery can often correct the problem, but it can be extensive, expensive, and painful, to say nothing of the time, expense, and pain of post-surgical rehabilitation.

While hip dysplasia is a hereditary disease, it can be exacerbated by rapid growth and exercise too vigorous for young, developing hips. Responsible breeders screen their breeding dogs using hip X-rays and only breed dogs whose family history indicates healthy hips. They also control the growth of puppies while they are in their care and provide feeding instructions for the new owners to maintain the slow growth rate that helps normal bone development.

Symptoms of Hip Dysplasia

- Bunny hopping when running
- Difficulty in the hindquarters when rising
- Walking with a limp
- A swaying gait
- Dropping the pelvis when the rump is pressed

Home and Lifestyle Treatment Hip dysplasia can be medically treated with canine NSAIDs and a joint chondroprotective. Appropriate exercise is important to maintain essential muscle support. Swimming is ideal because no weight is put on the joint while it's exercised.

A dog showing signs of lameness should be kept on a leash. As much as they want to play, most dogs ignore the pain and overdo it, which intensifies the lameness. Does this mean that dogs with HD can't play? They can, just not when they are going through a lame period. And play sessions, in general, need to be kept short and closely supervised. If she doesn't pull up lame the next day, let her rest for a day or two, and then allow her to play a

little longer the next time. Play and free walking let her go at her own pace, and the freedom of movement allows for greater muscle development.

Surgical Treatment As your dog gets older, surgery is often needed to relieve the pain and arthritis that accompany HD. The type of surgery depends on the severity of the hip dysplasia and the age of your dog. Generally, there are three surgical options:

- *Triple pelvic osteotomy (TPO)*: This procedure involves cutting the pelvis in three places to reposition the acetabulum (the socket), so that the femoral head (the ball) of the femur bone fits without slipping.
- *Femoral head osteotomy (FHO)*: The femoral head, the ball of the ball and socket joint, is removed, so that the femur and the pelvic bone are no longer in contact each other. The surrounding muscles must then support the leg. Physical therapy to strengthen the muscles significantly improves the outcome of this procedure.
- *Total hip replacement (THR)*: Both the femoral head and the acetabulum are replaced. Complete hip replacement, much like that for humans, is available for dogs with severe hip dysplasia.

Elbow Dysplasia

Elbow dysplasia refers to a group of elbow diseases. The most common are ununited anconeal process (a loose piece of bone within the joint), osteo-

89

chondritis (also known as OCD, which is cartilage damage within the joint), and fragmented coronoid process (a fragment of bone in the elbow joint).

The primary symptom of elbow dysplasia is front-leg lameness. Sometimes you may see a swelling of the elbow joint, often accompanied by a wider-than-normal stance.

Home and Lifestyle Treatment The home and lifestyle modifications for elbow dysplasia are very similar to those for hip dysplasia, with some important changes. It's critical to use ramps or steps to alleviate impact when the dog gets up or down from furniture or vehicles. The full weight of your Golden coming down on an already weak joint can cause more damage and a great deal of pain. Also, you need to eliminate activities that cause her to land on her front paws with any amount of force.

Surgical Treatment Surgery is often required for elbow dysplasia in order to remove bone fragments and to repair cartilage.

Heart Disease

In Golden Retrievers, the primary inherited heart disease is subvalvular aortic stenosis (SAS). SAS is a partial obstruction of the heart caused by an abnormally narrow opening between the left ventricle and aorta. This makes the heart work harder to pump enough blood to the body. The defect develops shortly after birth and worsens with age. It's often detected during a routine veterinary visit, when it's heard as a murmur, but diagnosis requires more advanced testing, as some murmurs will disappear as the puppy matures. In older dogs, exercise intolerance, fatigue, and fainting may all be indicators of the disease and dictate an examination by your veterinarian.

As mentioned, if your veterinarian suspects SAS, further tests will be needed. He or she may also recommend taking your Golden to a canine cardiologist. If the SAS is mild, special treatment may not be needed. Moderate to severe cases will require restricted exercise and possible medication. Balloon catheter dilatation can be used to increase the width of the opening.

Unfortunately, dogs with severe SAS usually have a shortened lifespan. The good news is that research to find the genetic markers for SAS is ongoing.

Epilepsy

The exact cause of epilepsy is unknown, but it is often attributed to an imbalance in the chemicals that transmit electrical impulses in the brain. A dog with epilepsy will usually begin having seizures anywhere between one and three years of age. The seizures are typically grand mal seizures and usually have three phases:

- **Prodromal phase (also called the aura or pre-ictal phase):** The first phase occurs hours or even days before the actual seizure and is characterized by changes in your dog's mood and behavior, such as attention seeking, hiding, withdrawing, restlessness, or apprehension. She may begin whining, trembling, running fearfully, and salivating.

- **Ictal or ictus phase:** Initially your dog's muscles will stiffen (this is called the tonic part of the seizure), causing her to fall on her side. This lasts for 30 seconds or less. With the onset of rhythmic motion, the clonic portion of the seizure begins. She may experience uncontrolled urination and defecation, profuse salivation, uncoordinated muscle activity, loss of consciousness, vocalization, and/or chewing motions. This phase can last from one to five minutes.

CAUTION

Poisons Can Cause Seizures

Some poisons can cause seizures that look very similar to epileptic seizures. If your dog has a seizure, call your veterinarian immediately.

- **Post-ictal or postictus phase:** This phase can last anywhere from a few minutes to a few days. Your dog may be disoriented, pace endlessly, eat and drink compulsively, be unresponsive, appear deaf or blind, or be hyperactive. Occasionally, because they are confused and therefore defensive, dogs in this phase can be aggressive.

Because seizures often occur while the dog is sleeping, you may not witness all three phases. Documenting the frequency and severity of the seizures will help your veterinarian to determine the best course of treatment for your Golden. A number of drugs are available to treat canine epilepsy; however, they are not 100-percent effective. The goal of these drugs is to reduce the severity and frequency of the seizures.

Eye Disease

If you plan to breed your Golden Retriever, her eyes should be tested annually to confirm that they are clear of any abnormalities and diseases. This testing—painless examination performed by a veterinarian certified by the American College of Veterinary Ophthalmologists—can be done through The Canine Eye Registration Foundation (CERF). This organization is "dedicated to the elimination of heritable eye disease in purebred dogs through registration and research" (*www.vmdb.org/cerf.html*). Owners of non-breeding Goldens don't need to have their dogs' eyes examined, unless their veterinarian recommends it.

Progressive Retinal Atrophy (PRA) Certain lines of Golden Retrievers are affected by an inherited eye disease known as progressive retinal atrophy (PRA). PRA refers to a group of diseases that cause degeneration of the retina; the result is declining vision and eventual blindness. Fortunately, breeders can now use DNA testing to identifiy dogs who carry the gene for one form of PRA, *prcd*-PRA, the kind that affects Golden Retrievers. A listing of tested dogs and their results can be found at *www.goldendna.com*. Breeders voluntarily add their dogs to the list to help buyers determine if the line they are considering includes affected dogs.

Pigmentary Uveitis Pigmentary uveitis, also known as Golden Retriever uveitis, is a progressive eye disease, where pigment appears in the front part of the lens. Although medication is available to help control the disease, studies show that 50 percent of Goldens with pigmentary uveitis will develop glaucoma and 33 percent will develop cataracts. Sadly, most dogs with glaucoma go blind.

If your Golden is affected by this disease, the Golden Retriever Club of America asks that you submit a blood sample to their research team or a DNA sample to the CHIC DNA bank.

Environmental Hazards

Intestinal Blockages (Bowel Obstructions)

The first thing that should be said about intestinal blockages is… *pick up your stuff!* Golden Retrievers are "mouthy" dogs, meaning that they like to have something in their mouths. The number-one cause of intestinal blockages is dogs and puppies ingesting things they find, often something smelly is stolen from the laundry basket or left on the floor. Since a dog's esophagus is larger than her digestive track, there's a high probability of an ingested foreign body causing a blockage in either the stomach or the bowels.

CAUTION

Toxic Plants and Foods

Many plants common to our gardens and homes (including dead leaves) can be poisonous to dogs. The ASPCA provides a long list of toxic plants at *www.aspca.org* under Animal Poison Control.

A list of toxic human foods can be found on page 64.

Symptoms If the intestine is either partially or completely blocked, the first symptoms are vomiting and a lack of appetite. A partial blockage can cause sporadic vomiting, diarrhea, or both over a course of weeks. If the blockage is complete, your dog may experience continuous projectile vomiting and won't be able to pass any stool or gas.

What to Do Take your Golden to the veterinarian immediately. An intestinal blockage can only be properly diagnosed with an X-ray. If a blockage is found, surgery will be required to remove it and repair any damage to the intestine.

Antifreeze

Be very careful when using antifreeze! Antifreeze has a sweet taste that dogs (and cats) like, and a very small amount is enough to kill your Golden Retriever. Immediately and thoroughly clean up any spills. If you think your Golden has ingested antifreeze, take her to your veterinarian or emergency clinic immediately. An antifreeze antidote called Antizol-Vet is available, but it must be administered soon after ingestion. Animal-friendly antifreeze is also available.

Hypothermia and Frostbite

When the seasons change, you really need to be tuned into your dog. Watch her behavior and look for signs of discomfort. This becomes even more important as your dog gets older or if she is under a year old.

Keep a closer eye on your Golden once the temperature dips below freezing. The colder it gets, the shorter the time you should allow her outside. At temperatures below zero, she should go out, do her business, and come back in the house.

Be sure to keep her well brushed, so that she doesn't mat. It's her undercoat that keeps her warm, so it must be kept in good shape. Keeping her nails, foot fur, and the fur between her pads trimmed minimizes the formation of painful snowballs between the pads.

If she is outdoors all the time, make sure she has an enclosed, raised shelter where she is completely protected from the elements, as well as a heated water bowl that won't freeze. Provide lots of good, soft bedding that she can huddle down into for warmth, and make sure vermin can't take advantage of this environment.

For an indoor Golden, keep an eye on her feet when she goes outside to play or for walks, especially if it's freezing and your neighbors are using salt and ice melt. Keep a damp washcloth near the door and wipe her feet off as soon as you get home. Salt can cause sores on the pads and ice melt can be dangerous if ingested. Booties are another option. Many companies now make great footwear for dogs.

Helpful Hints

Golden Snowballs

What should you do about the snowballs that form on your Golden's legs in the winter? Break them up with your fingers as best you can, and then gently pat her dry as the snow melts. This is also a good time to wrap your Golden in a blanket and snuggle. Watch her carefully to make sure that she isn't suffering any ill effects from the cold. Remember when your dog's fur is wet, it loses its ability to retain heat and keep her warm.

If you have a very young or aging dog, or it's very cold outside, I recommend some kind of jacket, preferably one that blocks the wind.

What are the signs that your dog is too cold? The most noticeable one is lifting her foot up and holding it above the ground. Check her ears and feet with your bare hands, because if they're cold, your dog is cold. Your dog may also start to shiver, a warning sign of possible hypothermia.

Also watch for signs of frostbite. In dogs, frostbitten skin appears red, purple, or gray. If it looks like your dog is suffering from frostbite, wrap her feet (or the affected part) in a blanket or towel and gradually warm her up; then contact your veterinarian.

Signs of hypothermia include violent shivering, non-responsiveness, disorientation, and stumbling. Most cases of hypothermia are the result of the dog falling through ice. If you are near a frozen lake, pond, or river, keep a very close watch on your Golden Retriever! If she is retrieving waterfowl in the late fall or early spring, the water will be cold, and repeated trips into the water may induce hypothermia. Make sure she has the opportunity to dry off and periodically warm up.

If your dog is showing signs of hypothermia, take her temperature. A dog's average body temperature is 101.3°F (38.5°C); if your dog's temperature is below 96°F (35.5°C), call your veterinarian immediately. If your Golden is suffering from hypothermia, you need to warm her, but not too quickly. Lying down with her and wrapping the two of you in a blanket is a good way to slowly warm up your dog.

HOME BASICS
Protect Your Golden Retriever from Heatstroke

- Never leave her in the car on a warm day. Remember, while the air outside the car may feel pleasant and cool to you, it doesn't take long for the interior of a car in direct sunlight to heat up to dangerous levels for your dog.
- In hot, humid weather, limit her exercise. Choose the cooler parts of the day for a walk and don't take her running.
- If she is outside, make sure that she is on cool grass and not asphalt or concrete.
- Ensure that she has access to shade and fresh, cool water. If you leave her in the yard while you are away, make sure the shade is continuous and doesn't disappear as the sun moves across the sky.

Heatstroke (Hyperthermia)

Unlike humans, dogs don't sweat. Instead, panting is a dog's primary method for cooling down. Because of their limited ability to cool themselves, dogs have a difficult time tolerating high temperatures.

Signs of Heatstroke

- Heavy panting and labored breathing
- Heavy salivation. The saliva will be thick and rope-like.
- Vomiting.
- Bright red (or pale grayish) mucous membranes and tongue.
- Disorientation or confusion.
- Difficulty walking or standing.
- Rectal temperature above 104°F (40°C).

What to Do

- First, if possible, move her into an air-conditioned building.
- Call your veterinarian and make arrangements to transport your dog to his or her office.
- Take her temperature every few minutes to determine when it has returned to normal. You don't want to overcool her, which can create a whole other set of problems.
- Try to cool your dog using cool water on her legs and trunk. Don't use cold water or ice, because they cause the capillaries at the surface of the skin to contract and inhibit the flow of cooled blood. Use a fan to speed the evaporation and cooling process; this gently cools the blood in the capillaries near the surface of the skin, and the circulatory system then transfers the cooled blood to the core.
- Don't force her to drink water.
- Make sure your dog isn't alone for any length of time until you can get her to the veterinarian. Heatstroke can bring on serious complications.

Caring for Your Sick Golden Retriever

It's inevitable; at some point in your Golden's life, she will have surgery or get sick and require your tender loving care. In this section, we will touch on a few of the important steps in canine recovery—feeding her, giving her medication, and making her comfortable. With your care and attention, she'll be up on her paws once again, ready for a new day of walks, pats, and snuggles.

Taking Your Dog's Temperature

Your dog's temperature normally ranges from 100°F to 102.5°F (38–39°C) with the average being 101.3°F (38.5°C). Canine temperature is taken rectally. Until you get used to taking your dog's temperature, it's best to have an assistant; one person to actually take the temperature, and the other to ensure the dog stays in a steady position. A digital thermometer works best and is the easiest to read.

Before you begin, clean the thermometer with alcohol and dry it off. Lubricate the end of the thermometer with petroleum jelly, and then lift the tail. With a gentle, twisting motion, insert the end of the thermometer into the anal canal, following the manufacturer's instructions.

Once you are finished, wash the thermometer thoroughly and disinfect it with alcohol.

Giving Your Dog Medication

At some point in your dog's life, you will probably need to give her some kind of medication. Many canine medications come in chewable, beef-flavored tablets, and most dogs gobble them up just like treats. But what if your dog is prescribed a drug that isn't available as a yummy beef chewable? Or if your dog is fussy and turns up her nose at the chewable tablets?

BE PREPARED! Supplies for an Upset Stomach

If your Golden has an upset stomach resulting in diarrhea or vomiting, it's always wise to have her seen by a veterinarian. If the veterinarian recommends a bland diet, try feeding her a combination of:

- Canned pumpkin puree (pure pumpkin, with no added ingredients)
- Rice
- Ground chicken or hamburger

Cook the rice and meat thoroughly, draining any grease from the meat, and mix it together in a bowl. You can store this in the refrigerator for two to three days. When you feed your Golden, give her a small amount of the rice and meat mixture and add about a teaspoon (5 mL) of the pumpkin puree.

If the medication is a chewable, the tablets can be cut in quarters so they are roughly the same size as kibble. Another alternative is to grind the tablets into a rough powder with a mortar and pestle, and then mix it into her food with a spoonful of plain yogurt.

But what about bitter-tasting pill? Your local pet supply store may carry a product designed to mask the bitter taste in a beef- or chicken-flavored wrap. Just put the pill into the wrap, close it up, and give it to your dog. She will think she is getting a treat.

Breed Truths

Watch Those Calories!

Remember, if you are using food to deliver medication, you need to watch your Golden's caloric intake, particularly for an ongoing medication.

Another idea is to hide the offensive pill in a piece of cheese, bread, or meat. However, your Golden has a keen sense of smell and may sniff out the pill, and then refuse to eat it. To get around your pill-sniffing dog, here's a trick that involves using three cubes of cheese to give one pill.

1. Give your dog the first piece of cheese, which will pass all inspections.
2. Next, give her the cheese with the pill while (and this is key!) holding the third piece of cheese right in front of her nose, so she knows another yummy piece of cheese is coming her way.
3. The middle piece of cheese with the pill in it becomes something she needs to consume in order to get to the next piece of cheese.

This method works almost every time!

Recovery

At some point in your Golden Retriever's life, she will inevitably get sick and require special care and medication. The instructions in this section assume you have already taken your Golden Retriever to the veterinarian and recommendations made by your veterinarian supersede any advice given here.

While she is recovering, a Golden normally kept in an outdoor kennel should be moved into the house so you can watch over her. Find a clean, warm, draft-free place for her. Take the opportunity to wash all of her bedding, so it's nice and hygienic for her. If your dog requires more warmth than regular household heat, discuss heating options with your veterinarian. For the safety of your dog, closely monitor any supplemental heating.

Your sick or recovering Golden should be kept quiet and calm, so care for her in a quiet part of the house, away from noisy televisions and children. Teach your children to be gentle and quiet around the dog when she is ill or sleeping. You must balance the need to care for her with her need to rest and be left alone.

Feed your Golden a nutritious yet appetizing diet. Unless your veterinarian recommends a change in diet, most sick Goldens do best on small amounts of the food they are accustomed to eating. Adding a small amount of good-quality protein, such as a hard-boiled egg, may aid recovery from serious illness. Her meals must be tempting enough to make her want to eat them, but light enough not to upset her digestive tract. If her veterinarian doesn't want her to return to her normal food immediately, but she is able to eat solids, then light, lean protein-rich foods are best for her. Fish, cooked eggs, or good-quality ground beef or chicken, with bland carbohydrates like mashed potato or cooked rice, are all good. Canned pink salmon with boiled potatoes is a good light meal to serve, or lean chicken with boiled rice. Your veterinarian may prescribe a specific diet, depending on what is wrong with your dog.

Remember, dehydration is a real possibility if your dog has been vomiting and has had diarrhea, so make sure that she drinks plenty of water. Your veterinarian may also recommend an electrolyte replacement solution. If she won't or can't get up, try placing a bowl of water under her muzzle. Gently dip your fingers into it and smear the water on her tongue or gums. Sometimes this will stimulate your dog to drink. You can also try spoon-feeding for water, liquid medicines, and non-salty meat broths.

As your dog recovers, follow your veterinarian's recommendations for resuming her normal daily activities.

Nutrition

As with humans, good nutrition is paramount to dogs' good health. There are several schools of thought regarding which diet is best for maximum health, and I recommend a conversation with your veterinarian to discuss the pros and cons of each. Every diet has its advocates and detractors, so it's important to do your research and come to an informed decision.

The subject of pet food can, and does, fill entire books, and I have listed some of my favorites in the Resources section. I encourage you to research this subject further and to make your own, informed decision based on what is important to you. Feeding your Golden is also discussed in Chapters 4 and 5.

Pet Food Standards

The Association of American Feed Control Officials (AAFCO) sets the standards for animal food's nutritional and ingredient composition. The organization is also active in setting the standards for pet food labeling, so consumers can easily discern the nutritional value of the food that they are purchasing.

The nutritional standards for pet food are periodically reviewed and modified. Dog food that meets the AAFCO standards fufills the minimum nutritional needs of your dog based on the following nutrients: protein, fat, vitamins, and minerals.

Understand the Label

The label of a dog food can tell you a lot about its contents. Every label is required by law to include the following: the manufacturer's name and address, a nutritional adequacy statement, ingredients, a guaranteed analysis, and feeding guidelines. Look for manufacturers who include a telephone number and a website or e-mail address. This information gives you easier access to company representatives. The nutritional adequacy statement on the packaging indicates the product meets AAFCO nutritional standards. This is important, because meeting the standards isn't required to sell dog food. Manufacturers who display the AAFCO logo have submitted their dog foods to long-term feeding trials to establish their nutritional claims. The nutritional adequacy statement must include the life stages for which the product is suited.

Ingredients

Pet food ingredients are not required to be FDA approved before they are marketed; however, the ingredients must be "generally recognized as safe" (GRAS) or approved food and color additives. I recommend looking for dog foods that use either USDA-approved ingredients or ingredients suitable for human consumption.

Ingredients are listed by weight in descending order. If chicken is the first ingredient listed, chicken accounts for the largest percentage of the content by weight. However, chicken is 70 percent water. When you compare that to dry ingredients, such as wheat or wheat gluten, that may be only 10 percent water, the wheat products may in fact contribute more solids to the food than the chicken. If there are multiple wheat products in a dog food, such as wheat flour, wheat middling's, and ground wheat, the individual wheat products may not outweigh the chicken; however, in aggregate, wheat may outweigh the chicken in that particular dog food.

Meal Meal is a concentrated form of protein and contains meat, skin, and sometimes bones. Look for single-source meal, such as lamb meal, rather than a generic meal, which could be from any kind of animal. Contact the food's manufacturer or check the website to find out what the meal contains.

By-products The AAFCO defines meat by-products as "the nonrendered, clean parts of slaughtered animals other than meat." This means that by-products can include internal organs, blood, brains, and, in the case of poultry, heads and feet.

Carbohydrates When it comes to carbohydrates, it's best to look for whole, unprocessed grains, such as brown rice, oats, barley, quinoa, amaranth, and millet. Unprocessed grains retain their nutrients and natural fats, and may be described as "meal" or "ground" on the package. Potatoes, peas, and sweet potatoes are also carbohydrates. Avoid fragmented products, such as middlings, grain fermentation solubles, bran, and flour, as these only contain part of the grain and thus are less nutritious.

Various fruits and vegetables are also used in dog foods to provide both vitamins and fiber—again, look for whole ingredients.

Preservatives Dog foods can be preserved using natural ingredients, such as vitamin E (mixed tocopherols); extracts of cloves, rosemary, and sage, and various forms of vitamin C, including ascorbic acid and ascorbyl palmitate. Avoid chemical preservatives, such as butylated hydroxytoluene (BHT), tertiary butylhydroquinone (TBHQ), ethoxyquin, and butylated hydroxyanisole (BHA). Also avoid foods that contain sweeteners and dyes, because they add no nutritional value and are not healthy for your dog.

Dog foods using natural preservatives will have a shorter shelf life than those using chemical preservatives, so always check the "best used by" date.

Types of Food

The most common kinds of dog food are commercially produced dry kibble (less than 20 percent water), moist food (65 percent water and generally packaged in cans), and semi-moist food (20–65 percent water and packaged in cans, foil pouches, or plastic wrap). All of these foods are designed to provide a single source of balanced nutrition for your dog.

Dog food manufacturers produce food for many different distribution companies. Look at the name and address on the packaging to make sure that it says "Manufactured by…" If the label reads "Distributed by…"

or "Manufactured for,…" you are not buying directly from the company responsible for the quality of the product.

Home-Cooked Food Home-cooked dog food is another option. Home cooking gives you a high degree of control over the quality of the food you feed your dog. However, it's imperative that you feed a balanced diet—and that means balanced for your dog, not for you. Canines have different nutritional needs than humans, and a home-cooked menu must meet those specific needs. Work with your veterinarian to make sure your Golden's home-cooked meals are nutritionally complete.

Prescription Diets If your Golden becomes ill, your veterinarian may recommend feeding her a diet specially formulated for her condition. Prescription diets cover a wide range of illnesses and conditions. Your veterinarian will tell you which formula is best for your ailing dog.

Water

A ready supply of clean, fresh water is essential for your Golden. Her water needs vary with her activity level and the season, so it's best to let her determine how much water she needs. Your job is to keep the water bowl clean and full.

It's a good idea to observe your Golden's drinking habits. Knowing what is normal for her will alert you to any radical change in her drinking pattern. Excessive drinking that is not caused by heat or exercise may be an early indicator of a medical issue, and she should be examined by your veterinarian.

Snacks

A treat like freeze-dried liver may sound gross, but it sends my dogs into spins of excitement. Veggies are also excellent treats for dogs. For easier digestion they should be parboiled, and then stored in the refrigerator. Fruit is best reserved for an occasional treat (for fruits to avoid, see page 64).

CAUTION

A Word About Raw-Food Diets

The subject of raw-food diets elicits strong opinions, both positive and negative. As with home-cooked diets, nutritional balance is critical. Feeding a raw diet also requires extreme cleanliness and meticulous preparation in order to avoid potential pathogens, such as *Salmonella* and *E. coli*. Additionally, studies have shown that dogs who are fed a raw diet shed both of these bacteria to a much higher degree than dogs fed a cooked diet. Therefore, dogs who are in contact with immuno-compromised people shouldn't be fed a raw diet. This is especially true for therapy dogs working in nursing homes, hospitals, and elementary schools.

Commercially prepared treats tend to have added sugar and dyes. And don't forget to include snacks and treats when calculating your dog's total caloric intake. This becomes very important when you are training a young dog and using treats as rewards.

Sometimes, just getting a bit of kibble from your hand is perceived as a treat. Often, it's not so much about the treat itself, but the positive moment you share with your dog when you give her something special.

Chapter Seven

Training and Activities

Training is a lifelong exercise. It can be a lot of fun, and at times completely frustrating. However, patience and consistency pay huge dividends; the tangible reward of a well-behaved dog, and the intangible bond between you and your Golden Retriever.

Training Wisdom

Your Golden Retriever thrives on consistency, and the most critical source of consistency in her life is training and commands. You may need to hold periodic family meetings to hammer out the commands everyone should use and to agree on which canine behaviors are acceptable. I can't reinforce this enough: It's vital all members of the family agree on the commands to use. If you or a family member is inconsistent, you confuse your Golden, and her behavior will reflect this confusion.

Once you agree on the commands and the acceptable behavior, enforce the rules. Saying "Oh, let her do it just this once," is a sure way to wreck the training program and confuse your puppy. It teaches her she doesn't always have to listen to you, which can be dangerous.

To begin with, treat your new puppy as if she were a full-grown dog. Why? Because your Golden Retriever will grow into a large dog, and what may be cute as an eight- to twelve-week-old puppy can turn dangerous when she is a large eight-month-old teenager. A small puppy isn't going to knock people over when she jumps on them; however, an eight-month-old dog can lay someone flat and potentially cause a serious injury. It is important she knows from the beginning what constitutes acceptable behavior.

Next, train her as if she were one of the more powerful breeds, such as a Rottweiler or a Pit Bull. If you haven't read it already, stop and go back to Chapter 2. I can't emphasize enough how critical it is that you understand how your Golden Retriever thinks. She is, first and foremost, a dog, and any dog—be it a tiny Chihuahua, a huge Mastiff, or your Golden Retriever—

FYI: Stop!

If you have skipped Chapter 2, please go back and read it. Before you embark on training your Golden, it is imperative that you understand how she thinks and how she views the world.

needs leadership, discipline, and training. Your Golden has all the potential to live up to the breed's reputation as a wonderful companion dog, but she cannot do it herself. If you don't provide her with firm, gentle leadership, behavioral problems will be a given.

Keeping your patience, taking a deep breath, and starting over will go a long way in your training. Remember, your Golden wants to please you more than anything else in the world, so it is up to you to be an effective communicator and to set her up for success. Not all training methods work with all dogs. If your Golden doesn't seem to get a certain command, you may just need to change how you are teaching it. Also, all training methods won't work all the time for your Golden.

Your mantra should be "Training, training, and more training!" At a minimum you will want to give her one to two solid years of obedience training. Your Golden Retriever is going to be a large, enthusiastic dog, so it is critical that she be well behaved.

Keep Directives Simple

One of the best things you can do for your Golden Retriever is to give her simple directives. It's counterproductive to chatter away at your Golden, thinking there is a command somewhere in there that she will understand, and then wonder why the poor, silly dog doesn't get the message. For example, if your Golden is in the flower bed, don't start shouting, "Sadie! Sadie! Sadie! What are you doing in there? You're stomping on my flowers! Get outta there!" All poor Sadie will get from the encounter is her name and the fact that you are angry with her for something about which she has no clue.

So how should you handle your Golden tiptoeing in your tulips? Take a deep breath, remind yourself the tulips will grow back next year, and in a calm, low, slow voice, tell her *"Sadie, out."* Use a hand signal to tell her which direction you want her to move in, and then, as soon as her back paws clear the flower bed, give her a *"Good girl!"* followed by lots of pats and sweet talk. (How to teach the *out* command is discussed later in this chapter.) Now, rather than being frightened and confused by what appears to be an arbitrary and irrational outburst on your part, Sadie calmly learns she isn't supposed to be in the garden and views the encounter as a training session for which she is rewarded.

Learn Different Training Methods

According to an old saying, "The only thing two trainers will agree on is that the third trainer is wrong." Needless to say, there are a lot of different training methodologies out there! Look for a training school whose methodology is based on positive reinforcement. There are a variety of positive training methods, and I encourage you to take multiple training classes, preferably with different instructors, so that you can pick up different perspectives and insights. Also, think ahead to possible jobs your Golden may have in the future and look for trainers who specialize in those areas. For example, if you plan to show your Golden, locate a trainer who specializes in performance training. Or, if you are going to work your Golden as a hunting dog, find a training facility or a club dedicated to teaching you and your Golden how to work as a team in the field. There are classes for just about every specialty, from agility to therapy work and everything in between.

Helpful Hints

Crate training and housetraining are addressed in Chapter 4.

It is also helpful to read books on dogs and dog training. (Some of my favorites are listed in the Resources section.) Having a variety of training methods at your disposal decreases your frustration and increases the productivity of your training.

Every Dog Has a Job

All dogs have jobs that require training beyond the basics of *sit*, *down*, *stay*, *walk*, and *come*. You may be thinking, "But my dog is just going to be a family pet and companion." Well, there is a lot for a dog to learn before she becomes a well-behaved family member, and only a small fraction of what she needs to know is taught in obedience class. Let's take a look at the training basics as well as the additional skills needed for some of the varied jobs held by Golden Retrievers, particularly the all-important job of being a well-mannered member of your family.

Keep Training Sessions Short and Positive

One of the most effective ways to train a dog is to use a reward-based training methodology.

Training sessions with a puppy need to be kept short, because puppies, just like kids, have short attention spans. If her attention wanders, close your session and make your next session shorter. Always end with a command she has mastered so she leaves the training session on a positive note. Young puppies work best in 30-second (yes, 30 seconds) to 2-minute sessions, so you need to have numerous short sessions each day. Keep the pace fast and fun so she greets each session with enthusiasm. As she grows, your puppy's ability to focus increases, so you can start to lengthen the training periods and reduce their frequency. That being said, training is an ongoing process, and you should take any and all opportunities to train her. For example, if your Golden wants to go outside, make her sit first, or, when you feed her, make her wait a moment before she can dive into her food.

CHECKLIST

Get Ready to Train!

You will need to have several items at hand when you begin a training session.

✔ A collar
✔ Two leashes, one 6-foot (2-m) leash and a 15–50-foot (5–15-m) check cord. (Retractable leashes are not good for training or walking, as they severely limit your control.)
✔ A clicker, if you are using one, or your enthusiastic voice!
✔ Treats, either in your pocket or in a bait bag clipped to your belt.

✔ A special training collar or head halter (usually only needed with leash training)
✔ Good posture (a straight back, with shoulders back)
✔ A positive, confident attitude. Your Golden can pick up on your mood instantly! Try to set aside the day's worries and focus only on her for a few minutes.

The Fundamentals

When you begin a training session, make sure to give your dog your full attention. Turn off the television, the radio, the cell phone, and any other distractions. Have your Golden Retriever wear her collar with her leash attached. Keep the treats in your pocket or in a convenient bait bag clipped to your belt. Using either a clicker or a verbal *"Yes!,"* instantly mark the correct behavior, followed immediately with a tiny treat. Eventually you can dispense with the treats at the end of each command, and your Golden will work for a click or a *"Yes!"* and get her reward at the end of the session. This training methodology is known as operant conditioning using positive reinforcement, and it is used to train a wide variety of animals, not just dogs.

Voice

Your voice is a very important tool when training your Golden Retriever. Not only is the tone important, but the cadence is as well. When working with your Golden, keep your tone and cadence appropriate to the command. For commands such as *come*, *heel*, *sit*, *down*, and *fetch*, your tone should be enthusiastic and the cadence fast and snappy. However, with commands such as *settle*, *stay*, or *gentle*, low and slow are your training watchwords. Why the differences? By changing the tone and cadence of your voice, you give strong, audible signals to your Golden Retriever.

Posture

Another critical element of training is your posture. You will need to stand straight, with your shoulders back, in a confident, non-threatening stance. I can't tell you how many times I forget this, only to have my dog ignore me. But, once I adjust my posture, that same dog snaps to attention and does as commanded. I'm not saying good posture is magic, but in my many years with dogs, I have found it remarkably effective.

Timing

The timing of the marker (the click or *"Yes!"*) and the reward is critical. You want to mark the behavior the instant it happens, and then give the treat. For example, when you tell your dog to sit, she gets a click or a *"Yes!"* the instant her bottom touches the floor, and afterward she gets the treat.

Breed Needs

Keep That Girlish Figure!

Initially the reward may be a food treat, but eventually you want to change it to either praise, a play session, or, the ultimate reward, a good belly rub or a pat. As discussed in the previous chapter, managing your Golden Retriever's weight is critical to her long-term health and snacks can really add up. During the initial period of intensive training, consider portioning out some of her daily food as a reward. A steady diet of treats is not good for her young digestive tract or her girlish figure.

When you first begin training your Golden you'll give the command as your dog performs the action. Take, for example, the command *sit*. Lure her into a *sit*, but wait until she finishes folding into the *sit* before you tell her "*Sadie, sit!*," mark, and then reward. She now clearly links the voice command with the action of sitting. You want to be 99.9 percent sure she is going to sit before you actually give the verbal command. By doing this, you set both yourself and your dog up for success.

Likewise, be ready to capture behavior as it happens. If you see your dog about to park her behind in a *sit*, tell her "*Sadie, sit!*," mark the behavior, and then give her a reward. Or, if she is running toward you, tell her "*Sadie, come!*," when she is almost to you, mark the behavior, and then give her a reward. Begin associating her natural behaviors (*down, come, sit, stay, watch*) with commands. This is a great addition to the other training you are doing with her and will help reinforce the commands.

Basic Commands

Sit

Sit is probably the easiest of all the commands to teach. Face your Golden Retriever, with the leash in one hand and a treat in the other hand. Place the treat close to her nose and then slowly move it over her head, luring her into position. As soon as her bottom touches the floor, tell her "*Sadie, sit!*," mark the behavior with either a click or a "*Yes!*," and then give her the treat and tell her she is a good girl!

Note: Never push down on her back end as this can be harmful to her hips. If she is experiencing discomfort when she is going into or coming out of a *sit*, it may be an early indicator of hip dysplasia. For more information on hip dysplasia, go to page 88. If you suspect hip dysplasia is the problem, see your veterinarian.

Down

The *down* command can be a tough nut to crack with your Golden Retriever. Her natural exuberance will likely have her popping out of position, her hind end in the air, tail waving! Capturing the *down* behavior as she naturally lies down is a great way to reinforce the desired action. Saving this command for later in the training session, when she is a bit tired, is helpful, because she will be more inclined to recline.

Lure your Golden into the *sit* position, and then slowly lower your hand to the floor between her front paws. If she does not lie down, move the treat *closer* to her body, between her front paws. If her back end pops up, place a very gentle hand on her back end (never push, as this can be harmful to her growing hips) to encourage her to keep it down. As soon as she is all the way down, tell her *"Sadie, down!,"* mark the behavior with a click or a *"Yes!,"* and then reward her with the treat and your praise.

Stay

When you are training your Golden to obey the *stay* command, two variables, time and distance, must be taken into account; one cannot be increased without adjusting the other. Remember, you are dealing with an exuberant dog who you want to set up for success. So, if you increase the length of time she is required to hold the *stay*, you must maintain a distance from her that she is comfortable with and at which she has had repeated success. For example, if she is successfully holding a stay for 30 seconds at a distance of 3 feet (1-m), you can increase the time to 45 seconds but keep the distance at 3 feet (1 m). Conversely, if you want to increase the distance, you will need to decrease the time. So, if she has been holding a 3-foot (1 m) stay for 60 seconds, you can move out to 5 feet (1.5 m), but decrease your time to about 15 seconds. Then gradually build back up to 60 seconds.

Let's begin. With your Golden on your left side, place her in a *sit*, give her the hand signal (fingers down, palm toward her), and then, in a low and slow voice, tell her *"Sadie, stay."* Leading with your right foot (left foot

Helpful Hints

Alternative Behavior Markers

Not everyone has the coordination, desire, or physical ability to work effectively with a clicker, but there are some very viable alternatives. If you choose to use your voice as your marker rather than a clicker, you must be absolutely consistent in your tone and cadence. A very quick and emphatic *"Yes!"* can serve as a marker. A clicking sound made with your mouth (think of the sound made to encourage a horse to move forward) can also serve as a marker. Whichever marker you choose—a clicker, a *"Yes!,"* or a vocally simulated clicker—the keys are consistency of sound and precise timing.

leading is reserved for walking), take two steps to the right, away from your Golden. If she tries to follow you, say "*No*" and try again. If she stays in her place, immediately mark the behavior, and then step back to her. Once she has the concept, gradually increase the length of time before you mark and reward the behavior, and then step back. If she has stayed in position for the duration of the exercise, mark and reward the behavior.

Leash Training

There is nothing more pleasant than a nice walk, with your Golden Retriever happily trotting along beside you, leash loose, and both of you enjoying a beautiful day. What isn't fun is having your dog drag you down the street

and wondering if your shoulder will ever be the same. You must train your Golden to walk nicely on a leash without pulling and to be responsive to your movements.

To begin, place your Golden on your left side and, in a happy and upbeat voice, tell her *"Sadie, let's walk!"* Then lead off with your left foot and start moving forward at a moderate pace. If her collar remains in the area of your knee for a few steps, mark and reward. Repeat every four to five steps.

If her collar moves past your knee, quickly change directions so that she must follow you. When she catches up to you, and her collar is once again even with your knee, mark and reward. What you are doing here is focusing her attention on your movements and rewarding her for maintaining proximity to you. As she gets older, you can allow her more latitude to explore, but as soon as the leash begins to reach its full length, it is time to change direction and her focus.

Helpful Hints

Walk Nicely

When teaching your Golden Retriever to walk nicely on a leash, practicing along a fence line will encourage her to focus on your movements.

Come

Your Golden Retriever has been bred to bring things back to you, which works to your advantage when training the *come* command.

Begin training your Golden puppy in a small area, such as a gated-off kitchen or a hallway with all the doors closed. Bend low or get down on your knees and call your Golden's name in a happy, upbeat voice. You can even try shaking her favorite toy or showing her the treat as an enticement to move toward you. When she is just about to you, tell her *"Sadie come!,"* and when she reaches you, mark and reward the behavior and tell her she is a very good girl. Rather than reaching out to give her the treat, make sure that she comes all the way to you. Make a big deal about her coming to

Fun Facts

"Here" Travels Farther!

Did you know the sound of the word *"Here!"* travels farther than the sound made by the word *"Come!"*? This is why field dogs are trained to come to the word *"Here!"* rather than *"Come!"*

you with a happy voice, belly rubs, treats, and anything else you can throw into the mix. You may feel a tad foolish doing this, but she should perceive coming to you as the best thing ever, and your excitement and enthusiasm are just what she needs as reinforcement!

If she needs more encouragement, put on her leash and gently pull her toward you. She will naturally pull back and resist at first, but once she is moving in a forward direction toward you, tell her *"Sadie come!,"*

111

ACTIVITIES AKC Canine Good Citizen (CGC) Certificate

Receiving CGC certification is a marvelous accomplishment for your Golden and a good starting point for the many fun activities and jobs that you and she can explore together. According to the AKC, "The Canine Good Citizenship Program is designed to recognize dogs who have good manners at home and in the community." CGC also promotes responsible dog ownership, requiring the owner to sign the AKC CGC Responsible Dog Owner's Pledge. The Canine Good Citizen test is comprised of ten individual skills, and your Golden Retriever must pass all ten before she can receive her CGC certificate. You will be restricted to using either a flat collar or a slip collar during the test.

Test 1: Accepting a friendly stranger — The dog will allow a friendly stranger to approach her and speak to the handler in a natural, everyday situation.

Test 2: Sitting politely for petting — The dog will allow a friendly stranger to touch her while she is out with her handler.

Test 3: Appearance and grooming — The dog will welcome being groomed and examined, and will permit someone other than the handler, such as a veterinarian, groomer, or friend of the owner, to do so.

Test 4: Out for a walk (walking on a loose lead) — The handler/dog team will take a short "walk" to show that the dog is under control while walking on a leash.

Test 5: Walking through a crowd — The dog and handler walk around and pass close to several people (at least three) to demonstrate that the dog can move about politely in pedestrian traffic and is under control in public places.

Test 6: *Sit, down*, and *stay* on command — The dog will respond to the handler's command: 1) *sit,* 2) *down,* and 3) *stay*.

Test 7: Coming when called — The dog will come when called by the handler. The handler will walk 10 feet (3 m) from the dog, turn to face the dog, and call the dog.

Test 8: Reaction to another dog — This test demonstrates that the dog can behave politely around other dogs. Two handlers and their dogs approach each other from a distance of about 20 feet (6 m), stop, shake hands and exchange pleasantries, and continue on for about 10 feet (3 m). The dogs should show no more than casual interest in each other. Neither dog should go to the other dog or its handler.

Test 9: Reaction to distraction — This test demonstrates that the dog is confident at all times when faced with common distracting situations. The evaluator will select and present two distractions.

Test 10: Supervised separation — This test demonstrates that the dog can be left with a trusted person, if necessary, and will maintain training and good manners.

and when she gets to you, mark and reward the behavior. Then, heap her with praise for being such a good girl. Practice this several times a day, each time increasing the distance, and soon she will come on command from any room in the house.

Once trained to come, she probably won't have many problems coming to you in the house. In the house, you are the most interesting thing to her. Outside, however, it's a completely different story. With all the potential distractions, you immediately lose your status as the most fascinating thing in her world. It's sad, but true.

When you are outside, I highly recommend having a check cord or a long leash on her at all times, until she is 100 percent reliable on the recall. Once your Golden knows the *come* command, you can add a hand signal, which is help-

Helpful Hints

If you want to show your Golden Retriever, I suggest that you find a training school that specializes in performance training. There you will learn the *heel* command, a very precise and exacting performance command.

FYI: Rescue Goldens and the Recall

If you have a rescued Golden, don't try to confine her in a small area with you as you would with a puppy, as she can perceive this as a threat. Remember, you more than likely don't know what her background is, and while she may seem friendly, she is getting used to a new place, new people, and, quite possibly, a new name. In a word, the poor girl is confused, and confusion makes us all a bit fearful. Until you know how she responds to enthusiastic commands, the best thing you can do with her is just sit quietly in a room together until she becomes comfortable with your presence. When she comes toward you, mark, toss her a treat and quietly tell her she is a good girl. As she gets very close, add the command "*come*," mark, reward, and tell her that she is a good girl. If you want to pet her, give her a scratch under the chin, not on the top of the head.

If you have a rescue dog, working with a leash or check cord in a fenced yard is an excellent idea, but you have to keep a tight hold on the leash or the check cord. As mentioned, until she settles in (which can take months) your rescue girl is a flight risk, and the best way for her to assuage her fears is to leap over the fence to freedom. Again, you want coming to you to be the best thing in her world, but with a rescue Golden it will take some time to establish that bond.

ful because it allows your dog to identify you from a distance. At the same time you tell her *"Sadie, come!"* put one of your arms straight up in the air and make a circular motion with your hand or full arm (depending on how far away your dog is), and continue to walk away, looking over your shoulder to check her progress. When she comes, mark the behavior and praise her as if she has just won Westminster! If you are working alone, give her a treat; however, if you are at a dog park, treats invite trouble with other dogs, so stick with effusive praise.

Because you always want to set your Golden Retriever up for success, do not tell her to *come* unless you are 99.9 percent sure she will come to you. If there is any doubt in your mind, go to her, snap on her leash or step on her check cord, pull her toward you, and when she begins to move in your direction, then tell her *"Come."*

Remember, one time does not make a trend! Training involves a tremendous amount of repetition, and repetition is the mother of skill. If you find that your Golden is not responding to your commands, you may be going too fast with her training. Go back to the basics and start rebuilding the foundation.

CAUTION

Restrictive Collars and Head Halters

If you have an untrained or minimally trained rescued or rehomed Golden, it may be necessary to use a training collar or a head halter for a period of time. Avoid using either of these until a need for more control arises, and then only with the supervision and instruction of a training professional. Such collars and harnesses should only be used when actively training.

A word on choke collars and other restrictive collars: Use them only when training, in conjunction with a normal flat collar, and with a great deal of caution. If you feel your Golden Retriever needs this type of collar in order for you to manage her, consult a professional trainer for instruction. Never leave any type of restrictive collar on an unattended dog. It is far too easy for the collar to get caught on something, and for your Golden to be seriously injured or killed.

The next two commands, *leave it* and *drop/give*, are invaluable to the Golden Retriever owner. As mentioned in Chapter 2, your Golden is bred to pick things up and carry them in her mouth, which, along with her keen nose, will lead her to put a variety of things between her jaws. Some will be okay, and others, well, I can pretty much promise you at least one or two freakout moments in the life of your Golden.

Leave It

Golden Retrievers are naturally inquisitive and, with their great noses, have an uncanny knack for finding disgusting things. Trust me, the first time your Golden Retriever employs her wonderfully sensitive nose to track down a rotting squirrel carcass, you will be very, very happy you taught her *leave it!* I just hope you can give her the *leave it* command before she proudly brings you this odiferous prize.

BE PREPARED! A Game You Don't Want to Play

When teaching the recall to your Golden, you want to have a measure of safety and control, particularly if you are outdoors, and this control is provided by the check cord. Used *only* with a flat collar (never with a collar that constricts the neck), a check cord is a straight piece of nylon cord, rope, or leather, ranging from 15 to 50 feet (4.5–15 m) long, with no loop for a hand grip (which can get caught on something). While some may suggest snapping a leash on a puppy who is not responding, this can unfortunately lead to the absolute best game in the canine world, Chase the Puppy. You *never* want to engage in this game with your Golden Retriever! You will never catch her, and it puts her firmly in the leadership position. Simply stepping on the end of the check cord lets you reel in your Golden if she finds something more interesting than you (gasp!) and is not responding to your commands. It lets you regain control of the situation without inciting a game of Chase the Puppy or becoming frantic because you're concerned for her safety.

It's important to remember that *leave it* means "walk away and leave whatever it is alone; you're not going to get it—ever." This is a very important distinction to make in your Golden's mind, because when she is going after the cat's food and you tell her *"Leave it!"* you don't want her to think she just has to wait a few minutes and then the cat food is once again fair game. This distinction impacts how you teach the command; you will need two different types of treats, one a little less tasty than the other. Keep the tastier one as the reward treat and use the less tasty one as the item to be left alone.

Holding her leash, place the less tasty treat on the floor and cover it with your hand. She will focus on the treat and may even nuzzle your hand trying to get to it. In your low, slow voice, tell her *"Sadie, leave it."* The moment she looks away from the treat, mark the behavior with a *"Yes!"* and then give her the super-yummy treat. (Pick up the treat on the floor so she does not get it. Remember, *leave it* means leave it forever.) The next phase is to put an uncovered treat in front of her, tell her *"Sadie, leave it,"* and then mark and reward her when she looks away from the treat. You want to make this increasingly difficult for her. Put her in a *sit/stay*, toss the treat about three feet in front of her, and tell her to *leave it*. Again, mark and reward her when she looks away from the treat.

You can then move on to teaching her to leave objects. Take several of her favorite toys or items that you know she would want to sniff (smelly socks come to mind) and set up a course in the yard or park. With your dog on her leash, walk her past the items, telling her to *"Leave it"* as soon as she notices one of the items. When she changes her focus and continues forward, mark and reward the behavior.

Give/Drop

While both are about getting your Golden Retriever to release whatever she is carrying in her mouth, there is a distinction between the *give* command and the *drop* command. *Give* means you want your Golden to release whatever she has in her mouth into your hand. Why is this important? Well, if you hunt with your Golden Retriever and she releases an injured bird before you have it in your hands, the bird can get away and prompt a rollicking game of chase the injured bird, which you don't want your Golden to learn to enjoy.

Drop, on the other hand, means to let go of whatever she has in her mouth and let it fall to the ground. This command is very useful for when she comes parading in with something nasty in her mouth that you would just as soon not touch. Most owners of Golden Retriever who are simply household companions will use the *drop* command for their games of fetch or if their Golden has, once again, raided the laundry basket.

Whichever command you choose or need to use, the training is essentially the same. Toss a toy for her (the *fetch* command is discussed in Chapter 10), and when she brings it back, offer her a treat. Then, as she either gives the toy to you or drops the toy on the floor, give her the *give* or *drop* command, mark the behavior with a click or a *"Yes!"* and then give her the treat.

Teaching Your Golden House Manners

Whether your new Golden Retriever is a puppy or a rescue, chances are good that you will have to teach her some manners. Manners for a dog? Really? Yes! Honestly, while the basic commands are important, we use the commands I am going to discuss shortly far more frequently. The basics are a great starting point, but on a day-to-day basis, they're not as useful as the commands you will learn in this section.

As you teach your Golden her house manners, there will be times when your voice is your only marker, and praise or a quick play session with a convenient toy the only reward. Why? House manners are trained in moments of opportunity, and, quite frankly, you're probably not going to have a clicker and treats in the pocket of your bathrobe at 5:00 A.M. If a training opportunity presents itself while you have your treat pouch and clicker on you, that's perfect; however, don't let the opportunity slip by just because the clicker and treat bag are not at hand.

Now, put on your Manners cap and let's get started!

Move

For a number of reasons, the most important and versatile command is *move*. Most of the time, your Golden Retriever will either be lying very close to you or in a high-traffic area of the house, where she can see the com-

CAUTION

Calling your dog to reprimand or punish her is one of the worst things you can do when training your Golden. Nothing will erode her trust in you more quickly.

ings and goings of the family. In our home, the landing at the top of the stairs is a popular hangout. Your Golden Retriever will be a big dog, especially when she is lying down, and she can move a lot quicker than you can. If you try to step over her, she will, in all likelihood, stand up while you are in mid-stride and send you flying. If she happens to be at the top of the stairs, you could go tumbling down the stairs. If she is in the kitchen, your head may get a painful introduction to the countertop. See where I'm going with this? It is much safer for you to condition her to move on command.

How do you teach her to move on command? Remember, she is a Golden Retriever, and retrieving is what she is bred to do, so use this to your advantage. When you find your Golden resting comfortably somewhere in the house, preferably in one of the high-traffic areas, grab a toy or a treat, walk over to her, and toss the treat or toy just out of her range. As she gets up to retrieve it (and she will!), in your low and slow voice tell her "*Sadie, move.*" As soon as she makes any kind of motion to get up or shift position, give her a click or a "*Yes!*" followed by her reward, either a treat or a hearty "*Good Girl!*" Eventually, she will only get the mark and reward when she actually moves her whole body out of your way.

FYI: That's My Name, Don't Wear It Out!

Your Golden Retriever's name is a critical component of your training; it is how you get her attention and, when other dogs are present, how she knows you are talking to her. Unfortunately, we tend to use our dogs' names too much, especially if they are family companions. For example, we mushy dog owners often sweet talk our dogs, all the while using their names, a situation made even more complicated when multiple family members do the same thing. What's wrong with that?, you may ask. The challenge for your Golden Retriever is making the distinction between the day-to-day chatter, which she can (and does) tune out, and a direct command. Your tone will make a difference to her, as will your posture, but if she has heard her name a hundred times that day, she may think it is just part of the daily background noise.

If this is the situation in your home, you can do one of two things. First, everyone needs to be very cautious about how frequently they use her name. For example, rather than saying "Who's my pretty Sadie girl?" instead say "Who's my pretty puppy girl?" so that she gets the sweet talk she loves, without the confusion of hearing her name for the hundredth time that day.

The other alternative is to give your Golden a name and a nickname, and then use her name only when training. For example, we call one of our dogs Wally in all our daily chattering, but, when we are serious and need his attention and obedience, we call him Wallace, which is the name used to train him. He tunes right in and obeys.

Ready/Watch/Her Name

Teaching your Golden to make eye contact on command to get her marching orders can come in very handy.

You can use the commands *ready*, *watch* or simply her name. To begin training, take a treat, hold it at the bridge of your nose, and tell her "*Sadie, ready.*" As soon as you have eye contact (it must be eye contact with you, not her eyes on the treat), mark the behavior with a click or a "*Yes!,*" and then give her the treat. Once she has mastered this, begin leaving your hand at your side and continue to mark and reward the eye contact. As she improves, increase the distance between you and the length of time that she has to maintain eye contact before she gets her mark and reward.

Off

Many people use the command *down* when they don't actually want their dog to lie down on the ground, but rather to get off of something, be it the guest who just arrived, the window ledge that she uses to see outside, or the sofa. To keep your Golden Retriever from becoming confused, it is important to make the distinction between the *down* and *off* commands.

Again, this command is trained in moments of opportunity. For example, if your Golden has just spied a squirrel outside and has placed her front paws on the window ledge for a better view, grab a toy or a treat, walk over to her, and toss the treat or toy just out of her range. As she moves to retrieve it (and she will!), in your low and slow voice tell her *"Sadie, off."* Once her front paws touch the ground, give her a click or a *"Yes!,"* followed by her reward, either a treat or a cheerful *"Good girl!"*

Breed Truths

Why Your Golden Needs House Manners

Why do I feel so strongly about teaching Golden Retrievers good house manners? I have had two rescues, both amazingly smart, sweet dogs, who came to us perfectly trained in the basics but without the skills needed to function within a household. In both cases, it was the lack of these skills, coupled with their natural exuberance, that led our beloved dogs to be surrendered to a shelter and a rescue organization. A Golden's inability to function within a home is very often why she is rehomed.

Stop the Jumping!

I have yet to meet a puppy who didn't try to jump on people. Couple that with the Golden Retriever's natural enthusiasm and love of people, and you have a recipe for jumping. This behavior can be cute when she is small, but as I stated earlier, it isn't cute when your fully-grown dog has just laid someone flat or soiled someone's clothes with muddy paw prints.

Here's how the training starts: Before company arrives, take your Golden for a good, vigorous walk. If your puppy is too young for a vigorous walk, a game of fetch to get rid of some of her puppy energy should do the trick.

Next, pick a spot 4 to 5 feet (1–1.5 m) back from the front door. Have her leash clipped to her collar, put her in a *sit/stay*, and step on the leash so that she can't get her head any higher than a normal *sit* position.

Mark and reward her for sitting nicely, and give her a special treat that you use *only* when guests arrive. Try some dried liver bits—disgusting to us, but candy for dogs. Have someone else answer the door, while you continue to manage your Golden. You may have to start off using the *watch* command, but every time her focus shifts from the guests coming in the door to you, mark and reward. Keep her focused on the mark, the treats, and your praise.

Now I'll be honest, you may need to practice this quite a bit before you can expect a calm puppy when people come into the house. For that reason, make guests coming and going from your home a regular thing, rather than a special event.

Another factor in this equation is how your guests react to your Golden puppy. When your guests first arrive, they need to ignore the puppy. Yes, I said ignore the puppy. (I know Golden puppies are the cutest things on earth, but this is important.) It will help with your puppy's behavior, because, if your guests convey excitement over the bouncing, jumping puppy, she will, in turn, react to it. Calm begets calm!

Gentle

As we have discussed previously, Golden Retrievers have an incredible zest for life; however, that high level of enthusiasm occasionally needs to be tamped down a bit—for example, when giving her a treat. While Goldens are known to have a soft mouth for hunting birds, it doesn't always seem so soft to fingers, and I'm sure you prefer giving treats without the addition of teeth marks to your fingers.

The nice thing about the *gentle* command is how easily it translates from one situation to the next. This command is more about an attitude you want your Golden to adopt, rather than an actual act you want performed. This same command can be used to preserve your fingers when doling out treats, or to keep your Golden from knocking down a small child with an over-enthusiastic greeting.

Your low and slow voice is the key to this lesson. (Think of the purr of a kitten rather than the bark of a dog.) Draw out the word so that it sounds more like *"Geeennntttaaalll."* Drawn out and said slowly, it sounds like the behavior you are encouraging in her. You are conveying the calm with your voice, and her verbal reward, *"Good girl!"* should be very low and drawn out as well.

Breed Truths

Depending on the temperament of your Golden Retriever, you may only need to work on this command a few times and she will have the concept for life, as has been the case with my two young males. Or, as with my senior female, you may need to remind her for a lifetime.

Begin by offering her a treat in your closed fist. Tell her *"Gentle"* as described, and then let her lick your hand to work the first open. If you feel any teeth make contact, give her a sharp, negative response such as *"Eh!," Eh!,"* and then remind her to be gentle. Offer the treat, tell her *"Gentle,"* and if you see an improvement in her approach, mark, give her the treat, and tell her *"Good girl!"*

You can also place the treat in your flat hand with an open palm, much like one feeds a horse. This will cause her to lick at the treat rather than use her teeth. You can even try smearing a little bit of peanut butter on your palm and letting her lick that off.

This command should be taught in small increments, until she approaches the offered treat slowly, with a closed mouth, and takes it with a nibbling motion.

Once she can consistently take a treat from you gently, begin applying the command to her greetings with people and other dogs, correcting her when she displays too much enthusiasm and marking all improvements. Remember, the *gentle* command is all about a shift in attitude. When she is playing too roughly, for instance, a calm *gentle* command can serve to quiet the situation. She isn't doing something wrong when you use the *gentle* command—just too much or too vigorously. For example, the curious puppy nosing a resident cat should be warned to be gentle. You want your Golden and the cat to get along—insist on it, in fact—so this is not a time for *"No."* An older dog who knows *gentle* understands what she is doing wrong if she gets too rough with a puppy. Likewise, the puppy who greets someone too rambunctiously can be verbally restrained with the *gentle* warning.

Out

If you have ever owned a dog, at some point you have probably been working in the kitchen, stepped back, stepped on her, and landed in a pile on the floor. Goldens want to be where you are and have an amazing ability to appear underfoot at the most inconvenient moments, particularly when there is food involved. The best way to avoid either of you getting hurt in these situations is to keep her out from underfoot. Dogs understand boundaries and limits, which helps when teaching your Golden Retriever the *out* command.

Because it is often the hub of activity, and the opportunity for tidbits to fall her way is very high, the most natural place to begin training *out* is the kitchen. This is easier if there is a doorway, but if you have an open floor plan, choose a boundary that keeps your Golden out of the way but still able to watch the activities of her people.

As with the *move* command, when you find your Golden Retriever underfoot and want her to move to a safer place, work with her natural instinct to retrieve things. Grab a toy or a treat, walk over to her, and toss the treat or toy just beyond the boundary that you have established. When she crosses the boundary, in your low and slow voice tell her *"Sadie, out,"* and then give her a click or a *"Yes"* followed by her reward, either another treat or a hearty *"Good girl."*

As you progress with this command, I recommend adding a hand signal. Ours is a simple sweep of the finger, ending with the finger pointed in the direction we want the dog to go. This can come in handy as reinforcement when you see her taking a tentative step across the boundary. It also helps if you have company and she begins to sneak back in; there's no need to stop the conversation to discipline her. Just a gentle, visual reminder to let her know you are paying attention and she can't sneak in for extra pats.

Make sure your boundary is very firm. Dogs being dogs, if you give an inch, they will, quite literally, take another, and the next thing you know, the boundary is well within the original limits. For example, in our home the boundary for the kitchen is the line between the kitchen flooring and the tiled hall. All of our dogs know they are not considered fully *out* until their front paws, toenails and all, are on the hall tile.

Once your Golden understands *out*, you can use it anywhere. For example, if you are outside and she is in the flower bed, tell her *"Sadie, out,"* give her the hand signal so she knows which direction to move in, and then a warm *"Good girl!"* as soon as her back paws clear the flower bed.

Golden Therapy Dogs

If you're lucky, you have felt the incredible sensation of stress melting away as your beloved dog greets you at the door at the end of a bad day. Dogs have a remarkable ability to ease stress and provide comfort. Sometimes people need more than a human touch to comfort them; they need the cold nose and warm heart of a dog to help them move forward. There is something intensely calming about the unconditional acceptance of a dog.

The Golden Retriever is especially adept at providing the calm, caring presence needed by people like a child struggling to read or a hospice patient seeking the courage to face his final moments. Studies have shown that the simple act of petting a dog can slow respiration, and the heartbeat, and reduce blood pressure. Studies have also shown that children who read to dogs see a significant improvement in their reading scores and overall academic performance. And it doesn't take a study to see the face of a sick child light up when the therapy dog comes for a visit, or the face of a nursing home resident grow soft with the memories of his own beloved dog, long since gone. Whether a

Breed Needs

Training Working Dogs

Interestingly enough, many of the training needs of hunting dogs are now shared by Golden Retrievers working as therapy dogs, assistance dogs, show dogs, or dogs just having fun at agility or obedience competitions. While they all need to be well-trained in the basics and well socialized with both people and other dogs, they also must be able to settle down on command, focus on their handler and be desensitized to noise. Instructions on how to train these valuable commands are discussed in Chapter 10.

therapy dog is changing a moment or changing a life, the power of a human and dog team is inspiring.

The first and most important requirement for a therapy dog is a gentle and reliable temperament. Your Golden Retriever must be friendly, outgoing, and imperturbable. Because of their natural exuberance, most Goldens aren't ready for active therapy work until they have settled into maturity at three to four years of age. If therapy work is something you want to do with your Golden, start her training early, have her CGC certified, and then begin taking therapy dog training classes, with the knowledge that you may need to repeat the class a few times before she is mature enough to go to work. Too many owners give up on the idea when their Goldens aren't sufficiently calm by age two, when a dog is generally assumed to be fully mature.

The Delta Society and Therapy Dog International, Inc., are two organizations that offer therapy dog certification. Once your Golden is certified, you will be assigned therapy visits according to your wishes and your Golden's special talents. While some dogs and owners have an affinity for children, others have the special something needed for the difficult work of hospice care. Other teams help people in shelters forget, if only for a few minutes, that life has dealt them a blow. The list of people whose lives can be positively affected by a therapy dog team is endless, and the need for therapy dogs grows greater every day.

ACTIVITIES Sports and Jobs for You and Your Golden

The Golden Retriever is an amazingly versatile breed, and the well-bred Golden has the smarts and the temperament to handle a wide variety of tasks. If you both have endless stamina, you and your Golden could hunt quail on Saturday, excel at an agility competition on Monday, and then go to work as a therapy team on Wednesday. Yes, Goldens are that versatile!

Sport/Job	Skills/Temperament Needed	Organization
Canine Good Citizen (CGC) Certification	The test is comprised of ten individual skills. (For details see page 112.)	American Kennel Club (AKC)
Therapy Dog	CGC certification is required, as well as therapy dog training. She must be friendly, outgoing, and gentle, have a reliable temperament, and be imperturbable.	Therapy Dogs International, Inc. The Delta Society
Retriever Field Trials	Field trials are competitive events.	AKC United Kennel Club (UKC)
Conformation/ Show Ring	Training for show dogs begins at a young age, and in this realm your breeder will be helpful.	AKC
Search and Rescue	The Golden Retriever's highly developed sense of smell, eagerness to please, and retrieval instincts make her a good dog for search and rescue work.	National Association for Search and Rescue, Inc.
Agility	Agility is a timed team exercise whereby the handler guides an unleashed dog through a series of obstacles. It is fast paced, great fun for both handler and dog, and a sport at which Golden Retrievers excel.	AKC UKC United States Dog Agility Association (USDAA) North American Dog Agility Council (NADAC)
Dock Jumping	Dock jumping requires the handler to throw a hunting dummy from a dock, and the dog to leap into the water to retrieve it. The dog with the longest leap wins!	AKC UKC DockDogs
Musical Freestyle	Dancing with your Golden? Why not? With a lot of training, coordination, and a love of dancing, you can both enjoy this activity.	World Canine Freestyle Organization Musical Dog Sports Association (MDSA)

Leash Training

1 In a happy, upbeat voice, tell her *"Sadie, let's walk!"* and then, leading off with your left foot, begin to move forward at a moderate pace.

2 If her collar remains in the area of your knee for a few steps, mark and reward. Repeat every four to five steps.

3 If her collar moves past your knee, quickly change directions so that she must follow you.

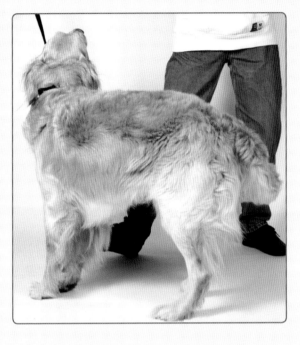

4 When she catches up to you and her collar is once again even with your knee, mark and reward, and then repeat step two.

The Sit Command

1 With a treat in your hand, face your Golden Retriever.

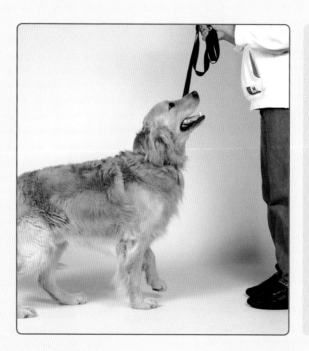

2 Tell her *"Sadie, sit,"* and then slowly move the treat close to her nose and over her head.

3 As soon as her bottom touches the floor, mark the behavior.

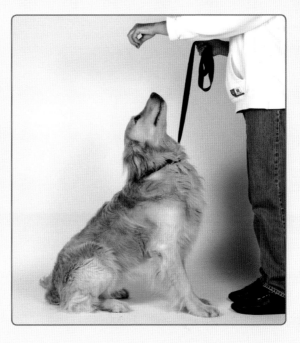

4 Give her the treat and tell her that she is a good girl.

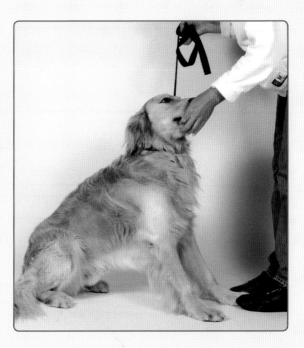

The Stay Command

1 Place your Golden in a *sit*, and then give her the hand signal (fingers down, palm toward dog) and the verbal command *"Stay."*

2 Take two steps away from your Golden, but retain your eye contact with her.

3 Slowly count to ten.

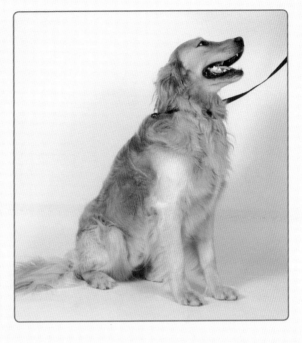

4 Step back to her. If she has stayed in position for the duration of the exercise, mark and reward.

Chapter Eight

Grooming

T here is nothing more splendid than the elegant plumes and feathers of the Golden Retriever coat gently floating in the breeze. In the canine world, the Golden Retriever coat is neither high nor low maintenance; it's somewhere in between. To enjoy her fabulous coat for years to come, you must understand its makeup and how to properly care for it. Because they were bred to retrieve waterfowl, Golden Retrievers have a dense, water-resistant double coat. The top layer of fur is coarse, oily, and water repellent, while the undercoat is soft and downy, designed to keep her warm. It is important to keep your Golden Retriever's coat in good condition, so she is protected from the elements. And beyond the luxurious coat, nails, ears, feet, and teeth need regular care and attention as well.

Bathing

Whether you hunt or not, her oily, water-resistant coat can sometimes give your Golden the distinct doggie odor of a hunting dog. Also, Goldens love the water and have an uncanny ability to locate mud and other nasty things to roll in. So learning how to bathe your Golden is important. Even if you take your Golden to a groomer, it is advisable to keep a bottle of canine shampoo and conditioner on hand; odds are, when your Golden decides to roll in something odiferous, it will not be when your groomer is available.

Choosing a Shampoo and Conditioner

There are a lot of shampoos on the market, and choosing the right one for your Golden Retriever can involve trial and error, not to mention expense. Generally, a mild shampoo and conditioner will do the job nicely.

There is also a wide range of specialty shampoos and conditioners that do more than just clean. For example:

- You can enhance the color of your Golden's coat by opting for a shampoo and conditioner made for light or red coats.
- Shampoos and conditioners designed for long or wavy coats help to make post-bath grooming easier and reduce the hair breakage that can occur when combing her out.
- If your Golden has sensitive skin or allergies, a mild, hypoallergenic shampoo and conditioner, or one designed for sensitive skin, can help

minimize her sensitivity to bathing. If she already has a rash, hot spots, or other sensitive skin conditions, consult your veterinarian for a recommendation as to which medicated shampoo is best to treat the problem.

- If your Golden has sensitive eyes, "tearless" shampoos are available.
- If fleas are an issue for your Golden, there are a variety of flea shampoos, some using chemicals and others containing natural botanical oils.

Helpful Hints

Placing your Golden in a *resting settle* (See Chapter 10, page 165) is a great way to clip her nails, check her paws and pads, and thoroughly brush her underside.

Before you bathe your Golden, give her a very thorough brushing and check for mats in her fur. Make note of the locations of the mats, so you can tease them out while she is wet using a detangling or spray-in conditioner. When mats get wet and are then allowed to dry, they become

BE PREPARED! Grooming Puppies and Rescues

Until she is used to the grooming routine and is comfortable with all parts of the process, keep a collar and leash on your Golden puppy or your new Golden rescue. Puppies are very squirmy, and a leash gives you more control. Rescue dogs sometimes need to be groomed before they have fully settled into their new homes, but a collar and a leash will keep your rescue girl from bolting from you. Both puppies and rescues require a gentle touch and a watchful eye.

Because a new owner seldom knows the history of a rescue Golden, caution is also needed when bathing, as she may have issues with being touched in certain places. A good time to begin to learn where she does and doesn't like to be touched is during your initial veterinary visit. Watch closely as your veterinarian runs his or her hands all over your rescue Golden, and study her carefully for any and all reactions. This way, you won't be surprised when you groom her for the first time. When you get to one of her reactive spots, have someone distract her with treats and praise while you attend to that area.

tighter and felted, making them more difficult to remove without damaging the coat.

You can protect your dog's eyes during bathing by using a sterile eye lube, available from your veterinarian. Also keep your hand over her eyes to prevent soap from getting into them.

To protect her ears, place your thumb over the ear opening to keep water out when rinsing. You can also insert cotton balls into her ears to help prevent water from entering and getting trapped in the ear canal. Don't forget to remove the cotton balls when you finish with her bath!

Place a rubber mat on the bottom of the bathtub and have your Golden hop into the tub. A handheld shower nozzle works best; however, a large plastic cup can also be used. Avoiding her face, start by thoroughly soaking her with lukewarm water, at the temperature that you would use for a baby or a very small child. Your Golden's skin, normally protected by her coat, is very sensitive. Apply the shampoo and gently massage it throughout her coat. Avoid scrubbing motions as this can tangle and damage her coat; gentle, non-circular motions are best. Rinse, apply the shampoo again, and gently continue massaging it throughout her coat, then rinse very carefully and thoroughly, making sure the water runs clear.

CAUTION

Hypothermia

To avoid causing hypothermia don't bathe your Golden outside with the cold water from the garden hose unless it is a warm day.

Apply the conditioner and massage it throughout her coat, again avoiding her face. While the conditioner does its work, take a damp washcloth (water only—no soap) and gently wash her face and inside her ears. This is also a good time to work out any of the mats that you may have found while brushing her. Then rinse the conditioner out of her fur. Softly squeeze the hair on the legs, tail, ears, and all other parts of the dog's body with your hands to remove excess water.

Helpful Hints

Want to avoid having your Golden shake while she is being bathed? Wait until the end of her bath to wash her head. Once her head is complete, hold up a towel and let the shaking begin!

It is critical that you completely rinse all soap and conditioner out of your Golden's fur. If any is left in the coat, it can cause skin irritations and hot spots, which can lead to a great deal of discomfort for your Golden and your wallet.

Gently towel her off (sponge towels work particularly well), avoiding circular motions that will tangle the fur. While she is air-drying, put some towels over her bed to keep it from getting damp and periodically replace them. It is important she does not lie down on damp towels—or, for that matter, her own damp fur—for long periods of time, as this can cause acute moist dermatitis, also known as hot spots. Make sure she is kept in a draft-free location, and if it is cold outside, keep her indoors until she is completely dry. If you choose to use a dryer, you must towel dry her first. Do not use a conventional hair dryer on your Golden, because even the lowest setting is too hot. Use either a special canine dryer or, forego the use of a dryer and use absorbent towels.

SHOPPING LIST

Grooming Supplies

- ✔ Canine shampoo and conditioner
- ✔ Waterproof collar and leash
- ✔ Lots of old towels
- ✔ Canine-specific hair dryer
- ✔ Nonslip rubber mat for the tub
- ✔ Good-quality pin brush
- ✔ Slicker brush
- ✔ Steel comb
- ✔ Mat cutter

- ✔ Scissor-style nail trimmer for large dogs
- ✔ Styptic powder
- ✔ Toothbrush and toothpaste
- ✔ Blunt-nose trimming scissors
- ✔ Ear wipes (for maintenance)
- ✔ Ear wash and cotton (for deep cleaning)

HOME BASICS
Bathing Your Golden in the Family Tub

If you plan to bathe your Golden Retriever in your family bathtub, these tips will help you prepare, stay safe, and minimize the mess.

- Place a rubber mat on the bottom of the tub so that she doesn't slip.
- Make sure to place a non-slip mat outside the tub, or to wear non-slip shoes. (Trust me, there is going to be water outside of the tub.)
- Lay out all of your bathing supplies within easy reach, so that you can maintain contact with your Golden throughout the entire process. If you have to grab something that you forgot, leaving your wet Golden in the tub, chances are good you'll return to find a soaking-wet bathroom or at worst, a wet dog, shaking and romping around the house.
- I can almost guarantee your Golden is going to shake, probably more than once! Expect to get wet and the fur to fly—everywhere! Don't be surprised to look up and find it on the ceiling.
- So you don't have to wash it later, remove the shower curtain.
- Lay a towel over the sink area and put away all counter items, especially toothbrushes.
- Expect to do a thorough cleaning of the bathroom, including the walls, after the bath.

137

Brushing

As mentioned before, it is important to keep your Golden's coat in good condition, and brushing is a critical part of coat care. Be sure to brush through both the rougher top coat and the downy undercoat. If the undercoat is not regularly brushed and detangled, it will mat. The most common areas to mat are the neck (also known as the ruff), the ears, under the arms, and the backs of the legs.

Regularly check your Golden's ruff and ears for mats after play sessions, because play biting and wrestling can cause large, deep mats.

Your Golden is going to shed—a lot! This can be mitigated to a degree by frequent brushing and by using an undercoat rake. The change of seasons often increases the level of shedding, which calls for more frequent brushing.

Brushes Are Important

The quality of the brushes you buy makes a big difference to your Golden and the comfort of her grooming. The two primary brushes that you will use are the pin brush and the slicker brush.

A pin brush has metal tines with rounded ends. When purchasing a pin brush, look for one with rounded ends cast in metal rather than plastic caps. The reason for this is twofold. First, the plastic caps can fall off, leaving a sharp metal edge that can scratch your Golden's delicate skin. Second, the

FYI: Mats—How They Form and How to Deal with Them

A mat is a tangle of hair that has formed a very tight knot. It is often so tight, it is impossible to brush or comb out normally, and requires special attention and tools.

How do mats form? Hair is covered in tiny scales that act as barbs, locking hairs together when they are tangled. These scales also catch all manner of dirt and debris, forming a solid mass of hair that is nearly impossible to untangle—a mat.

The Golden's water-resistant double coat, with its coarse, oily layer on top and the fine, downy undercoat beneath, make the Golden particularly prone matting, especially around her ears, ruff, underarms, hindquarters, and the anal area.

If you don't regularly and thoroughly brush out your Golden's coat, mats will develop. Some people deal with mats by simply cutting them out, but this leaves unsightly gaps in the coat. If you find a mat, it is best to take the time to carefully break it apart so the appearance of her coat isn't damaged.

The first step in mat removal is to have the proper equipment; preserving the coat requires specific tools and hair care products. You'll need:

- *Oil-based coat conditioner spray*: The oil in the spray smoothes the scales on the hair, loosening the mat so that it can be combed out more easily and with less hair breakage.
- *Mat comb*: This comb-like tool has blades instead of teeth and is used to slice mats into smaller, easier-to-handle work sections.
- *Sharp scissors or a mat splitter*: Sometimes, when undetected, mats can grow very large, and the best way to begin tackling a large mat is to cut it into strips with scissors or a mat splitter.
- *Slicker brush and steel comb*: After cutting the mat into smaller parts, you'll comb out the mat with the sturdier steel comb and then go over it again with the finer slicker brush.

If you find a mat in your Golden's coat, first spray it with a detangler or a spray-in conditioner, and then try to comb it out, starting at the outer edge and working in small sections back toward her skin. If this doesn't work, you may need to use a mat cutter to break up the mat. Once the mat is broken up, thoroughly comb out the area with the steel comb and then again with the finer slicker brush. This process requires a bit of work, but it is worth the effort to avoid the ugly gap in her fur that cutting out the mat with scissors can cause.

plastic tends to catch in the hair, rather than glide through it, and can cause painful pulling. While a pin brush with rounded metal ends will be more expensive, it is well worth the investment.

A slicker brush is a tool with tines made of thin wire, which can be sharp, mounted on a soft, flexible backing. Slicker brushes designed specifically for shedding have tines set at two different heights. Slicker brushes are usually square or rectangular in shape. It is wise to test pressure levels on your own arm before using the brush on your Golden. While the slicker brush does a lovely job of cleaning out the dead fur and giving your Golden's coat a nice, finished appearance, it can also damage her skin if used improperly.

Beginning with the pin brush, give your Golden a gentle, all-over brushing. The pin brush will pull out most debris and quite a bit of loose and dead hair, so you will need to clean it frequently.

Next, rebrush her with the slicker brush. Remember, this brushing cannot be as vigorous as the one done with the pinbrush. Brushing with a slicker brush requires extra care, as it is very easy to scratch the skin. Short, gentle strokes are better than long, hard ones. Also, avoid the head, face, and ears, as the skin in these areas is just too sensitive for the slicker brush. Slowly move the slicker brush through her fur, keeping the pressure light and working in the same direction the fur is growing. The slicker brush will pick up the loose hair that the pin brush missed, and it will also need to be cleaned out frequently.

Hot Spots

Unfortunately, the Golden Retriever's heavy, double-layered coat puts her at risk for acute moist dermatitis, also known as hot spots. Hot spots are moist, hot, wound-like areas, 1 to 4 inches (2.5–10 cm) in diameter that develop rapidly, often in a matter of hours, and can be very painful. A variety of things can trigger hot spots, such as fleas, allergies, irritants, infections, or poor grooming. Hot spots often appear prior to a heavy shedding period, when dead hair and moisture get trapped against the skin. Frequent brushing can be a huge deterrent to the development of hot spots. Also, make sure your Golden is completely dry after bathing or taking a swim, particularly during hot, humid weather, because having wet fur against her skin for a prolonged period of time can create a hot spot.

Breed Needs

Avoiding Warts and Lipomas When Brushing

As she ages, your Golden will probably develop various lumps and bumps, the most common of which are warts and fatty lipomas. Before you begin brushing your old girl, give her a thorough once-over with your hands to identify any raised areas on her skin. (New lumps and bumps should be seen by a veterinarian.) Brushing can irritate or injure anything protruding from her skin, so carefully brush around these protrusions. Once you have brushed her everywhere else, take a comb and very gently comb the fur around and on top of the bump. Why a comb rather than a brush? A comb impacts a very small area and gives you more control while working these delicate areas.

Hot spots grow and become infected when they are repeatedly licked and scratched. Initially your veterinarian will have to treat the hot spot. Depending on the size of the hot spot and the degree of pain your Golden is experiencing, she may have to be sedated in order to be treated. The veterinarian will clip or shave the fur around the hot spot, gently cleanse the skin, and allow it to dry. The hot spot will need to be treated for 10 to 14 days with a topical cream or powder, and possibly a course of antibiotics or corticosteroids. Your veterinarian may recommend an Elizabethan or similar collar to prevent her from further irritating the hot spot while it heals.

Nails

Keeping your Golden Retriever's nails trimmed and in good condition is critical to the health of her joints. Nails allowed to grow too long will cause a dog to walk with an unnatural gait, which stresses the joints all the way up the leg. Nails that are too long also tend to get caught on things and break, which is extremely painful for your Golden. And don't forget the dewclaw! It's very prone to getting caught and tearing.

The nail is made up of the hard material on the outside (keratin) and the fleshy, pink quick on the inside.

Using a scissor-style nail clipper, nip off the end of the nail, making sure you do not nick the quick. If you own a Golden mix, and her nails are black, you will not be able to see the location of the quick. If you turn her paw over, however, you will see an indentation leading from the tip back to the quick.

If you do happen to clip the quick, you can stop the bleeding with styptic powder or, in a pinch, some flour. Pack the end of the nail with the styptic powder until it stops bleeding, and then keep her quiet for a while so the nail doesn't start bleeding again. Put her in her crate or confine her to an uncarpeted room, such as the kitchen, for a little while.

Squirmy puppies can be taught to enjoy nail trimming by employing the mark and reward system taught in the previous chapter. If you are using a clicker, put the treat under your thumb, on top of the clicker. Begin by holding her tiny paw and tapping the end of her nail. Each time she is non-reactive, she gets a mark and a reward. When she is regularly non-reactive to tapping the ends of her nails, begin introducing the clipper, nipping just a tiny bit off the end of the nail. Again, mark and reward for non-reactive behavior.

Many dogs are reluctant to have their feet touched, which makes trimming nails a bit of a challenge. This can be particularly true of rescues, because there may be a previous paw injury you don't know about. You will need to slowly accustom your rescued Golden to having her feet touched before you can begin trying to trim her nails. It may take a while for her to learn to trust you, and you may have to take her to the veterinary clinic or a groomer a few times before you have established enough of a bond for you to trim her nails.

If you are at all unsure about trimming your Golden's nails, I highly recommend getting a lesson from a professional groomer or your veterinary technician. If you are still not comfortable after this, most veterinary clinics trim nails for a nominal fee.

HOME BASICS
Nine Steps to Healthy Golden Ears

In all my years with dogs, I am still surprised at how fast their ears can get dirty! Make a habit of giving her ears a quick flip and peek every day to make sure they are in good condition. The L shape of the canine ear canal makes it a prime collection point for dirt, debris, and fluids, all of which can cause irritation and infections. Lifelong ear maintenance is critical for your Golden, especially if you want her to hear you sweetly calling her name well into her senior years.

(Caution: *Never* use cotton swabs in your Golden Retriever's ears!)

1. Examine your Golden's ears daily. Lift the ear flap and check for waxy discharge, buildup of dirt or blood, and red or inflamed skin (basically, anything other than clean, healthy-looking skin.)
2. While you have the ear flap up, take a quick sniff to make sure there is no odd or foul odor emanating from the ear, as this can be an indicator of an irritation or infection.
3. Make sure the hair in the ear canal is trimmed. Long hair in the ear canal can act as a magnet for dirt, bacteria, allergens, and moisture, creating a breeding ground for infection. If you notice the hair is longer than ¼ inch (6 mm), carefully trim it with a pair of blunt-nose scissors, ensuring the hair doesn't fall down into the ear canal.
4. Trimming the fur under the ears increases the flow of air and keeps them drier, helping to mitigate potential infections.
5. Pre-moistened ear wipes are okay for a quick cleanup of the outer ear, but they cannot take the place of a thorough,

deep cleaning with ear wash, which gets much further into the ear canal, where infections begin. The frequency of full ear cleanings depends a lot on your Golden's lifestyle and general health. Every Golden needs to have her ears deep cleaned after a swim or a bath to remove any water that may have found its way into the ear canal.

6. To safely clean the ear, soak cotton gauze in a squeeze bottle filled with a solution of 40 percent vinegar and 60 percent water, or in a premixed solution recommended by your veterinarian. Gently wipe the ear clean, manipulating it so you can see into all of the nooks and crannies.
7. Using a fresh piece of solution-soaked gauze, very carefully wipe into the opening of the ear canal to clean inside. Check the gauze; if it comes out clean, and you didn't detected any odd or foul smell earlier, you are done. However, if you did notice an odor, or the gauze comes out with any gunk on it, you now need to clean the ear canal. Using the squeeze bottle, gently send a steady stream of ear wash into the ear canal. This loosens and removes ear wax, dirt, and dead skin that has built up there.
8. Let your Golden have a good shake, which moves the cleaning solution and the debris it has loosened up and out of the ear canal. You may need to re-wipe and dry the outer ear area.
9. If redness in the ear persists or a rapid reaccumulation of debris occurs, your Golden may have an ear infection and should be seen by your veterinarian as soon as possible.

Teeth

Yes, your Golden Retriever needs dental care! As with humans, a buildup of plaque on her teeth can lead to infection and other health issues. Along with a good diet, brushing her teeth two to three times a week keeps her teeth in tip-top form. Chews approved by the Veterinary Oral Health Council (VOHC) are also a great way to help keep your Golden's teeth pearly white.

Feeding a diet that includes hard kibble is helpful in removing tartar from the teeth, but only if your Golden actually chews the kibble. If she swallows her food whole, the kibble will have no effect on the tartar and plaque buildup on her teeth.

Check your Golden's teeth frequently to make sure that they are all in good working order. A broken tooth or an abscess on the gum line can be both painful and dangerous for her and will require immediate veterinary attention.

How do you brush your Golden's teeth? First of all, you must use a special canine toothbrush and canine toothpaste. If you take a look at your Golden's teeth, you can't help but notice that they are significantly larger than human teeth, hence the special toothbrush. The two most popular

CAUTION

Do Not Use Human Toothpaste on Your Golden's Teeth

Human toothpaste can contain the artificial sweetener xylitol. This common sugar substitute causes hypoglycemia (low blood sugar) in dogs, as well as acute and possibly life-threatening liver disease. A very small amount can produce toxic effects in your dog. After ingesting xylitol, dogs may begin to vomit and develop hypoglycemia within 30 to 60 minutes. Even worse, some dogs may develop liver failure within 12 to 24 hours.

versions of the canine toothbrush are one that looks like a human toothbrush but with a wider head, and a finger toothbrush that slips over your index finger. You can also use a washcloth or a piece of gauze to finger-brush her teeth. The special toothpaste is necessary because your Golden doesn't have the ability to rinse and spit like we do, and human toothpaste is not meant to be ingested. Also, canine toothpaste, tastes better to dogs (thanks to chicken or beef flavoring) and is specifically designed to address canine plaque and tartar.

Begin by letting your Golden lick some canine toothpaste off of your finger so that she is familiar with the taste. Then, again using your finger, rub some toothpaste on her gums in a circular motion, so that she begins to get used to the motion and the feel of you working in her mouth. Apply the toothpaste to the brush and begin brushing just the outer side of her teeth, working close to the gum line where plaque builds up. A quick brush is all that is needed, followed by loads of praise, and some treats or play. She will gradually relax when having her teeth brushed, and as she does, you can brush more thoroughly, working up to cleaning the inside of the teeth.

Even with your best efforts, your Golden may still need to have her teeth professionally cleaned by your veterinarian from time to time. This is done under anesthesia.

What can happen if you don't brush your Golden's teeth? Again, much like humans, she can develop periodontal disease, which can have a very negative impact on her health over the long term.

CAUTION

Electric Clippers

If you plan to use electric clippers when trimming your Golden, read all of the instructions that accompany the clippers very carefully. Better yet, arrange to take a lesson or two from a professional groomer or someone with extensive experience using electric clippers on Golden Retrievers.

Trimming

Unless you plan to show your Golden Retriever, trimming is very limited. The most important parts to keep trimmed are her feet and rectal area.

The fur in and around the feet should be trimmed regularly, along the top, below, and between the pads. Trimming your Golden's paws is as important as trimming her nails. Begin by clipping the hair around the bottom of the paw so that it is level with the pad up to the nails. Then, using your finger, bring the hair up from between the toes to the top of the paw and round it to the shape of the paw. Turn the paw over and, using short blunt-nosed scissors, carefully trim the fur from between the pads. Trimming the fur between the pads is particularly critical if you live in a region where it snows in the winter or is hot and humid in the summer. In the winter, snow gets trapped in the fur between the pads and develops

into painful snow or ice balls. In hot, humid summer weather, moisture can get trapped in the fur between the pads, causing itchy, painful hot spots. Finally, trim the fur on the back of the leg from the heel pad up to the stopper pad.

If you notice a reddish change in color on your Golden's paw, it may be caused by persistent licking due to either an allergy or some sort of irritation. Check her feet and, if necessary, call your veterinarian.

Keeping the hair in her rectal area trimmed short helps prevent fecal matter from catching in her fur. This is of particular importance as your Golden ages or if she develops joint issues, because she may not be able to squat enough for the fecal matter to fully clear her coat. Begin by gently trimming all of the fur, including the underside of her tail, about an inch (2.5 cm) away from the anus. If you still find fecal matter in her coat, you may need to increase the trim area or shorten some of the plumes on her legs, tail, or both. If you take your Golden to a groomer, this is known as a sanitary trim.

Breed Truths

Should you shave your Golden in the summer? Unless she has an exceptionally thick coat, a very active lifestyle that may cause her to overheat, or is continuously in woods or fields where she picks up a lot of burrs, I don't recommend shaving her. Her coat provides critical protection for her sensitive skin.

Chapter Nine

The Senior Golden Retriever

I must confess, I have a special place in my heart for senior dogs. There is something extraordinary about our relationships with senior Goldens. Gone is the bouncy enthusiasm of youth, and in its place is a steadfast, quiet companionship that is without parallel. You both know every nuance of the other's being and character, and words almost become unnecessary. A gentle pat or the soft swish of a plumy tail speak volumes. The gray on her muzzle and face begins to mirror your own as you both move through life, content in each other's company. Walks are slower as time takes its toll, but the air is sweeter and the sun is brighter, because you share them with a longtime friend.

The subject of senior dogs and their care can, and does, fill entire books. Some of my favorites are listed in the Resources section. If you have a Golden who is entering her geriatric years, I encourage you to do more reading and research on the subject, so you and your Golden can enjoy many more delightful years together.

Physical Changes

While it may seem like just yesterday your Golden was a puppy, time marches on very quickly. Even if she doesn't act it, your Golden is clinically classified as a geriatric or senior dog at around age eight. At this point in her life, when changes in her health happen more rapidly, her annual veterinary visits become twice-yearly visits. Your veterinarian will likely recommend a baseline senior workup that includes a complete blood panel and chemistries, urinalysis, liver and kidney functions, parasite examination, and thyroid check.

As mentioned in Chapter 5, you want to get touchy-feely with your Golden to check for any changes, but once she reaches her senior years, your once-a-week checks should become daily or every-other-day routine. Given the high incidence of cancer in Goldens, early detection is critical. Remember, as she ages, changes happen a lot faster than when she was young.

Exercise Needs

As she gets further into her senior years, exercise with your old girl will change, but it is still critical to her overall health. The more active she has been during her life, the better off she will be in her senior years. What used to be a brisk, hour-long walk may become two half-hour strolls each day. As she ages and slows down, monitor her reactions carefully. If you go for a walk and she is lagging behind for the last half, make tomorrow's walk shorter. If she lies down to rest on the way home, maybe tomorrow should be a short stroll around the block. Trust me, it is not fun carrying home a large, over-tired dog, or trying to coax along an old girl who just wants to lie down in the grass and take a nap. While it's important for your aging Golden to get daily exercise, it is equally important not to overdo it.

Like all seniors, human or canine, your senior Golden will have good days and bad days so it is up to you to moderate her activities. On her good days, she may go like a house afire, but you know she will pay for it later, so temper some of her enthusiasm. It is very tempting to just roll with it when your dog of yesteryear suddenly appears! But trust me, the heartache the next day, as she struggles to get up off of her bed, will take your breath away. Let her have fun, but don't let her get carried away.

Conversely, your arthritic old girl is going to feel better if she gets some exercise every day, so even if she's a bit creaky, get her moving, if only for a walk around the backyard. There is a tremendous amount of truth in the old saying "Use it or lose it," and if you don't keep your old girl moving, she will lose her mobility. If she is struggling with joint issues,

consider using a support harness to help her move; she continues to work her muscles, and you get to work on your biceps.

Hearing Loss

Much like humans, dogs gradually lose some of their hearing capabilities, usually beginning around age 10. Most dogs do not have a total loss of hearing and can hear if you yell loudly, whistle, or clap to get their attention. If your aging Golden seems to be losing her hearing, you can retrain her to hand signals (with the same training methods you used to teach the verbal commands) and modify your lifestyle to accommodate her new limitations. First and foremost, always keep her on a leash, because if she wanders off, she will not hear you calling her. (Even if you don't hunt, please read "Breed Truth: Aging Hunting Goldens" to the right for a good tip on getting your deaf Golden's attention.)

Breed Truths

Aging Hunting Goldens

Hunting dogs can lose their hearing earlier in life than other Goldens due to lifelong exposure to the ear-damaging volume of gunshot. If you have trained your Golden to work to hand signals, you are ahead of the game when she begins to lose her hearing; however, she isn't going to be able to hear you call her to know when to look for those hand signals. To solve this problem at home and in the field, get a vibration collar (not a shock collar!) and train her to look at you when she feels a buzz.

To avoid startling the old girl, don't touch her while she is asleep or if she doesn't know you are there. For example, if she is standing by the door looking out into the yard and hasn't looked back to see you approach, don't come up from behind and touch her. The best thing to do is to stamp your feet on the floor to create a vibration, so that she can feel, rather than hear, you approach.

Not all hearing loss is due to age. If you notice your Golden's hearing is not what it used to be, don't assume it is due solely to aging. Take her to the veterinarian to rule out a possible ear infection, a response to an antibiotic, hypothyroidism, or some other cause.

Vision Loss

Vision loss can have many causes, and it is always best to take your Golden to the veterinarian if you notice diminishing visual acuity. Beyond the normal eye issues of aging, such as glaucoma and cataracts, a loss of vision can also be an indicator of certain cancers.

If your old girl is losing her sight or has lost most of it, first and foremost you must keep her safe. When you cannot be home to supervise her, make sure that she is in her crate or a confined area. She has a mental map of your home, so help her out by not moving any of the furniture and keeping hallways and pathways clear of obstructions. It may look like she is getting around fine, but she doesn't have echolocation like a dolphin, so if you move the chair, the poor old girl is going to bump into it and possibly injure herself.

Put a gate across the stairs and keep the cellar door closed. Don't allow her to go up or down stairs unless someone is with her. If you do not have a fenced yard, she can no longer go outside without supervision, because if she wanders off, she will not be able to find her way home. To that end, put a special tag on her collar stating she is blind, in case she is ever lost.

Don't give up on her exercise. Just because her eyes don't work doesn't mean the rest of her doesn't! She can continue her daily walks and activities but she may need you to use your voice as a homing signal. So chat with her while you walk; you know you have a lot to say to her!

Behavioral Changes

Behavioral changes in your senior Golden are often directly linked to the physical changes she is experiencing as she ages. What may appear to be a negative change in her attitude can actually be an indicator of pain. Hesitation to go outside or enjoy something new, or barking at

CAUTION

Think Twice About the Boarding Kennel

When you travel, your old girl may be less tolerant of going to the boarding kennel than she once was, so consider having a friend come and stay at the house with her. Staying in her home is less stressful than going to a strange environment, even if she has been to the boarding kennel in the past.

family members, may indicate a decline in her visual acuity. And not coming when called or being startled when you walk up behind her may point to hearing loss. Bring any changes in your Golden, either physical or behavioral, to the attention of your veterinarian.

Diet and Grooming

It is critical that you keep your senior Golden lean. It improves her mobility, allows you to feel any new lumps and bumps that may appear, and most importantly, prolongs her life. Geriatric dogs typically need 30 percent fewer calories due to their decreased activity level. As your Golden slows down, you will need to cut back on her calories, but do not cut back on the quality of the food. Many senior dog foods have a reduced amount of protein, but unless your geriatric Golden is on a protein-restricted diet, these foods can actually be detrimental to her because they do not provide enough protein to maintain her muscles. In fact, studies show healthy senior dogs benefit from a high-protein diet, which allows them to maintain muscle tissue.

If you have been feeding your Golden once a day but need to reduce her calories, consider feeding her two or three times a day. This will help her maintain her energy more evenly throughout the day and reduce the chances of her trying to scavenge extra food from inappropriate sources. If your Golden is overweight, work closely

Managing Change

Your aging Golden is less adaptable to change, so alterations in her daily routine need to be made slowly. Visitors, particularly children, should approach her slowly, handle her gently, and understand if she decides to walk away from them. While your Golden may not want the attention of strangers, she will find great comfort in being in the company of her family. Make sure her bed is near the hub of the family's activities.

with your veterinarian to put together a safe weight-loss program. Older dogs should not lose weight rapidly; reduction should be limited to no more than 1.5 percent of her beginning body weight each week. A drop in calories can mean a reduction in essential nutrients, so don't be surprised if your veterinarian recommends a vitamin or mineral supplement.

Your Golden's digestive system may become more sensitive as she ages, so make any dietary changes carefully and with the help of your veterinarian. Certain medical conditions require special diets, and prescription foods are available through your veterinarian.

Senior Grooming

As she ages, your Golden's coat will get thicker and curlier, requiring more attention and grooming. It also makes it more difficult to feel any changes in her skin, so check her diligently. Her nails need to be trimmed more frequently because she is less active and isn't wearing them down as much as when she was younger. And chances are good she can't execute

FYI: Canine Cognitive Dysfunction Syndrome (CDS)

Canine cognitive dysfunction syndrome (CDS) is a progressive, degenerative brain disease similar to Alzheimer's disease in people. While it is relatively common in dogs over the age of ten, a diagnosis of CDS catches many owners by surprise. Knowing the indicators of CDS will help you to identify the symptoms early. Because all of the behavioral changes associated with CDS can also have their source in other physical ailments, it is important to work with your veterinarian to rule out other causes. If the diagnosis is CDS, it is treatable with a drug called Anipryl (selegiline hydrochloride, L-deprenyl hydrochloride), which is used to treat Parkinson's disease in people. While about a third of all dogs do not respond to the drug, disease progression is slowed significantly in one third, and dramatic improvements in symptoms can be seen in the remaining third.

The symptoms of CDS are varied and may show up individually or in multiples. When a symptom appears, it is often simply chalked up to old age and dealt with as needed, until another symptom appears. In order to get an early diagnosis and put your Golden on a treatment plan, it is critical that you know and look for the signs of CDS specifically:

- A change in sleep patterns. Goldens with CDS sleep more than normal, especially during the day, and are very restless at night, often pacing and acting confused.
- Changes in interactions with the family. A previously friendly dog may become withdrawn and behave as if she doesn't know her family members. Or a Golden who has, until this point, not displayed any neediness may want 24-hour contact.
- Soiling in the house. She may no longer remember where she is supposed to eliminate.

- Failure to respond to commands or her name (if deafness has been ruled out).
- Personality changes. For example, a Golden with an outgoing, friendly personality may become timid or aggressive.
- Random barking for no obvious reason, particularly at night. This often happens with CDS because she is confused by the darkness. It can also happen if she gets "lost" in the backyard or gets stuck in a corner.
- Pacing or anxiety. Dogs with CDS will sometimes just wander aimlessly around the house, unable to settle down.
- Separation anxiety. Dogs who have never had an issue with being left alone may suddenly experience separation anxiety symptoms. (This was how we learned our beloved Kayleigh had CDS.)
- General confusion. There can be many indicators of confusion, including not recognizing you, getting stuck in corners, standing on the hinge side of the door when she wants to go out, getting stuck behind or under furniture, or just standing and staring into space for long periods of time.
- Changes in appetite. Dogs with CDS sometimes forget to eat.

Working with your veterinarian, you can help to improve your Golden's cognitive abilities through antioxidant dietary supplements, increased mental stimulation, and, if needed, medication. With aggressive treatment, your old girl may be able to return to her former self and continue to enjoy her senior years. Having had a dog with CDS, I can assure you that nothing is better than seeing your old girl's plumy tail waving happily again!

the perfect squat when defecating, so trim the area around the anus to keep fecal matter out of her fur (see page 145).

Keeping Your Aging Golden Comfortable

Geriatric dogs often need special gear. Orthopedic beds provide support for aging, arthritic joints. Also, depending on where you live, you may want to consider a heated bed for your aging Golden. Seniors are very sensitive to temperature changes, and keeping her warm in the winter and cool in the summer help her mobility and quality of life.

At a minimum, you want to invest in a ramp to help your aging Golden move easily in and out of your car, which saves her joints from the impact of jumping and saves your back from the task of lifting her. If she is used to sitting on the furniture with you or sleeping on your bed, consider getting

CHECKLIST

Physical and Behavioral Changes to Watch for in Your Senior Golden

Changes in your Golden's physique and behavior can be the harbingers of deeper health issues, so if you notice any of the following, consult your veterinarian.

✔ Changes in appetite, either an increase or a decrease

✔ Changes in weight

✔ Increased thirst

✔ Increased or decreased urination

✔ Changes in bowel movements, including, constipation and diarrhea

✔ Abnormal discharge containing pus or blood, emanating from the eyes, ears, nose, mouth, anus, vagina, or penis

✔ Fever

✔ Paleness of the gums and/or tongue

✔ Panting when not hot or for extended periods of time

✔ Rapid or labored breathing

✔ Fatigue and exercise intolerance

✔ Coughing

✔ New lumps or bumps

✔ Any kind of sore

✔ Hair loss, either in a given spot or an overall increase in shedding

✔ Hearing difficulties

✔ Cloudiness or an unfocused appearance of the eyes

✔ Aggression

✔ A change in sleeping patterns

✔ Confusion

✔ Incontinence

✔ Separation anxiety

✔ Unexplained barking

her a set of stairs so she can easily climb up and down. Though it may seem like a very short distance from the couch to the floor, the impact on her joints can be debilitating over time.

There are a plethora of slings, harnesses and carts available to help keep your aging Golden mobile. Your veterinarian and care team can help you decide which one is best for your dog at the moment. At the moment? Yes, break out your wallet, because as she ages, the gear she needs changes.

Medications

Just like humans, elderly dogs often take one or two prescriptions along with several vitamins and supplements. Everyone in the family must be clear on how and when these are administered to her. I would suggest writing it all out and keeping the instructions with the medications. (Keep all canine medications and supplements out of reach of children.) You never know when an emergency may require a neighbor to feed and medicate your elderly Golden, and written instructions will make it easier for you, your neighbor, and your dog.

(Information on how to give your Golden medication can be found on page 96.)

Helpful Hints

Dietary Supplements

Work with your veterinarian to add joint-enhancing supplements to your senior dog's diet. Glucosamine and chondroitin supplements can make a tremendous difference in her mobility. Also, natural anti-inflammatories, such as fish oil, can stave off the need for a prescription anti-inflammatory, which can be hard on her liver and kidneys.

The Last Tail Wag

When you start to see the ever-increasing gray on your Golden's muzzle and watch her lag behind on her walks, it's a terrible reminder that the lives of our dogs are too short. Someday in the not-too-distant future, you may have to make the decision no one wants to make. Although we may never talk about it, we all secretly hope that, when the end comes for our beloved Golden, she will quietly pass away in her sleep, Nature having made the decision for us. But, with all the advances in canine health care, dedicated owners often have to face the reality of a beloved dog's diminished quality of life and to decide if bringing her life to a gentle close is the best thing for her.

Hospice

With hospice care, your Golden can spend her remaining time in the comfort of her own home rather than in a clinical environment. Talk to your veterinarian to find out if this is something he or she offers or if he or she can provide a referral to a canine hospice organization.

Euthanasia

Euthanasia is when a veterinarian puts a dog to sleep using an overdose of anesthetic. It is quick and painless, and the dog does not suffer. When your old girl is no longer getting any joy or pleasure out of life, or is in constant pain and unable to do the things she loves, it may be time to put her down. In the last days of her life, it doesn't matter if she eats all the yummy stuff that once was so bad for her. Let her eat the treats loaded with sugar and fat. Her last days should be all about saying good-bye and enjoying a few last pleasures.

If you know that the end is near, make arrangements, if you can, for your veterinarian to come to your home so that your Golden can pass away in familiar, peaceful surroundings. If it isn't possible for the veterinarian to come to your home, either ask to wait in your car at the clinic or see if they can provide you with a quiet room and a comfy floor cushion, so you and your old girl can share a few final moments.

It may be the most difficult thing you will ever do, but honor your beloved companion and be present when she leaves this world. She has been true to her Golden Retriever heritage and has made you the center of her universe; return the devotion and let your face, your tender touch, and your loving voice be her final memory of this world.

Grieving

Grief is a natural reaction to losing a loved one. Not only natural, it's critical that you mourn the loss of your beloved Golden. She was a member of your family for the duration of her life, and you never made a decision without considering the impact it would have on her. She was not just a dog, but a friend, a treasured companion, and a confidant. Give yourself permission to fully mourn her passing and allow yourself to feel all of the emotions associated with it.

Children often react differently than adults to the death of a pet. As a parent, you need to help them understand the permanence of death and let them know their beloved Golden is not coming back. Often, children do not have the right words in their vocabulary to explain how they feel, and art can be a wonderful form of expression for them. If you have children, I highly recommend the book *Saying Good-bye to Your Pet* by Marge Eaton Heegaard, which is listed in the Resources section.

If you are having a difficult time coping with the death of your Golden, ask your physician or veterinarian for a referral to a bereavement counselor, who can help you cope with the loss of your dog. Many humane societies offer pet loss support groups, where you can be among others who have also lost a treasured pet.

Capturing the Memories

When your beloved Golden passes away, designate a special notebook or album to record your memories of her and add your favorite photos. In the days, weeks, months, and even years after she passes away, you will fondly remember certain moments in your life together. Write them down, and when you start missing her, open your notebook and relive the rich and wonderful life you had together.

Breed Truths

Yes! You Can Skip Right to Senior Dog Bliss!

Hard as it is to believe, not everyone is enchanted with puppyhood. But how do you skip puppyhood and the lengthy time it takes for Goldens to mature? Rescue! For any number of reasons, Golden rescue organizations always have older, mature Goldens available for adoption. Often (but not always) these dogs are beautifully trained, have the perfect, sweet Golden temperament, and are just waiting to live out their golden years in a forever home.

Chapter Ten

Preparing Your Young Golden to Hunt

We can't cover everything about training a hunting dog in one short chapter, but I can give you some helpful tips for getting off to a good start with your new hunting Golden. Many of her inbred talents can be enhanced by working with her at home until you can begin more formal hunting training. A number of specialized schools will train your hunting dog, and bring you in at the end of the training to teach you as well, but they can cost thousands of dollars. Even if you're a rookie, you are certainly capable of training your dog yourself by working through breed clubs, your local GRCA, hunting training clubs, formal obedience training clubs, and experienced hunters. You can develop a network of resources and use that network to find a hunting training mentor.

Begin at the Beginning

Preparation begins by working with a breeder who specializes in breeding Goldens for the sole purpose of providing superior-quality hunting dogs. He or she should actively hunt the Goldens, as well as compete in field trials and other hunting-related competitions in the off-season.

As mentioned in Chapter 3, hunting Goldens are usually bred to the smaller, lighter side of the breed standard. A breeder of hunting Goldens selectively breeds the traits necessary to make them exceptional in the field—namely, a stable, focused temperament (so that they remain steady to wing and shot), a strong-willed personality with a high level of intensity and energy, a keen nose for both flushing and retrieving game, and high intelligence. A dedicated breeder of hunting Goldens will also begin to teach and condition the pups for field skills.

How do you locate a breeder of hunting Goldens? Word of mouth is a good way to begin. Ask your hunting friends with Goldens, or those who

BE PREPARED! Special Rules for Hunting Puppies

When training a hunting dog, you must be careful about the behavioral associations she makes.

- Get her wet, early and often. While you don't want your kids to stomp through puddles, you do want your Golden puppy to, even if it means cleaning up a mess. Because she is going to be in all sorts of conditions and weather when she is hunting—not to mention lakes, rivers, and streams—she needs to get used to the feel of wet feet and being in the water. Letting her splash around in the shallows (make sure the swimming area is completely free of obstructions) is also a great way to acclimate her to being wet, but keep a tight grip on the check cord attached to her collar so she doesn't swim off.
- Don't tug. Why? The last thing you want is for your Golden to get the idea that, when you hold out your hand to take something from her mouth, it is a game. Tugging games also encourage aggression, which is never a good idea with any dog.
- Avoid squeaky toys. Small animals squeak when caught and you do not want your Golden associating any game she catches with a toy. If she has stuffed toys with squeakers, get out your sewing kit and perform a squeaker-ectomy.
- Don't let her eviscerate stuffed toys. Again, you do not want her thinking she can do the same to a perfect pheasant she has just retrieved. To develop and encourage her soft mouth, tell her, low and slow, *"Be nice"* or *"gentle"* when she is being overly enthusiastic with a stuffed toy.
- Avoid command confusion. For example, the word *mark*, depending on the context, has two different meanings: 1) a command for the dog to visually lock onto a bird; and 2) in a duck blind, a word used to tell a hunting partner about incoming waterfowl. For example, *"Mark, west"* lets the partner know that birds are flying in from the west, without having to make any movements. If you regularly use the term *mark* with your hunting partners to indicate incoming waterfowl, you do not want your Golden to jump up and get ready to work! You may want to choose another word, such as *look*, as the command when you want your dog to visually lock onto a bird.
- Expose her to future hunting environments. Take your hunting puppy exploring in environments that closely replicate the places you like to hunt, so she can get used to tall grasses, trees, and scrub, and the noises associated with being in the field.
- Be careful about socialization. It is critical that your hunting Golden be well socialized, but she needs to know not every interaction is a party.

know other hunters who have Goldens, where they got their pups. Again, this is a good way to start your research, but by no means is it the end; be sure to read Chapter 3. Getting referrals from your local hunting or gun club, or talking to Golden owners at field trial events, will also net you some good leads, but it is critical you do your due diligence.

We all know a hunter who has spent all sorts of time and money to purchase and train a hunting dog, only to figure out she doesn't have a good

nose or is a bit too high-strung to be steady to shot. Hopefully, these dogs become beloved house dogs, while the hunter again begins the process of looking for a hunting partner. Is there ever a 100 percent guarantee? No, but doing your research and working with a committed breeder with a proven track record of producing champion field dogs is about as close as you will get.

Basic Obedience Training

All hunting dogs need a rock-solid foundation in the basic obedience commands. Plan to enroll her in obedience classes as soon as she is fully vaccinated and cleared by your puppy veterinarian. (To give her a head start, begin at home using the information in Chapter 7.) Some training schools, particularly in the Midwest, offer obedience classes specifically for hunting pups, and it would be worth your while to locate one in your area, if available.

Helpful Hints

Field Trial Retiree

A great way to get a perfectly trained hunting Golden is to find a field trial competitor who didn't come out on top, and whose owner wants to make room in his or her competition group for an up-and-coming potential champion. What do you get out of this? While not a champion, you'll get a highly trained Golden who will likely make a fabulous hunting companion.

Rescues Can Be Trained to Hunt!

Don't overlook rescue organizations as a potential source for your future hunting Golden. Golden rescue organizations that foster their dogs get a real feel for the temperament and strengths of a given dog, and there are Goldens in the system with all the potential in the world to be fabulous hunting dogs. Talk to the rescue organization and let the staff know you are looking for a Golden who can double as a family and hunting companion. Chances are good you will meet with success!

Early Hunting Training

Is eight weeks too young to begin training and conditioning your hunting Golden? Not at all! Hopefully, your breeder has already been working with the litter. Just remember, until she is about nine months old, everything associated with hunting should be fun. You are setting her up for a lifetime of enjoyment working as a team. You want her whining with excitement every time she sees you reach for your hunting jacket.

When she is very little, work with puppy dummies, and then move to full-size dummies and decoys at around six months.

Fetch

As soon as you bring her home, start in a closed-off hallway and toss a toy, wing, or other retrievable item down the hall. When she has it in her mouth, very enthusiastically call her name, pat the floor, and

generally make a big deal of it. Introduce the word *fetch* as she gets to you, and then say *"Good fetch, Sadie!"*

At nine weeks, give her only two fetches at a time, and then gradually increase the number, but always stop the game early to leave her wanting more. Remember, she isn't going to get unlimited retrieves in the field, so she needs to learn to relax in between throws. Repeatedly throwing a ball or training dummy for her does not train her to chill out between retrieves.

It is important to vary the items, so she gets used to the feel of different things in her mouth. Toys, wings, puppy training dummies, magazines, slippers, keys—pretty much anything that will fit in her mouth and not hurt her.

Give

Timing is important for this exercise. Have some treats in your pocket, and when she brings back the fetched object, bring a treat out for her to see and smell. Watch her closely, and as she begin to releases the object, tell her *"Sadie, give."* Once she has released the object, give her the treat and a very enthusiastic *"Good girl!"*

Hold

Getting her to give the bird isn't as much of a challenge as having her continue to hold the bird until it you can take it. Holding is important because the dog may think re-chasing the injured bird she has just dropped is a very fun game. To get your Golden to continue to hold the bird, start to run the other way so she begins to chase you. Naturally, she will catch you, and when she does, quickly turn, say the *give* command, and take the bird.

Developing a Soft Mouth

The Golden Retriever is categorized as a soft-mouth retriever, but it is up to you to develop and encourage this talent early in her life.

Begin her training with feathers or wings as soon as you bring her home, so that she gets used to the feel in her mouth. Then, working with training dummies and wings, wrap two wings around a dummy with baling wire. This won't hurt her, but she won't like the feel of the metal against her teeth (think of your teeth striking the tines of a fork), so she will naturally loosen her hold to avoid the sensation.

Helpful Hints

No Bird

Your Golden is a bird dog to the core, which is great when you are in the field. But there will be times when she sights a bird and you do not want her to visually lock onto it—say, at a field trial or when she spies your mother-in-law's parakeet. It is important to call her off with *no bird*. You can train this in much the same way as you train *ready/watch* (see Chapter 7). When she spies a bird and locks onto it without a *mark/look* command, tell her *"Sadie, watch, no bird."* And as soon as she has shifted her attention and you have eye contact with her mark the behavior with a click or a *"Yes,"* and give her a treat. As she improves, drop the *watch* from the command and simply say *"Sadie, no bird."* Then direct her to another activity.

Scent Training

Place commercially available scent on a training dummy, hide it in the yard, and then bring your Golden pup out of the house. Place her in a *sit/stay*, let her get a good whiff of the air, and then tell her *"Fetch!"* (Only do this exercise if you have a fenced yard; otherwise, keep her on a very long check cord.)

To make this even more difficult, wait until nighttime, place one drop of scent on a tennis ball, place her in a *sit/stay*, and throw the ball far into the dark and then tell her *"Fetch!"* (Only try this if you have a fenced yard.)

Mark/Look

Because a Golden's eyesight is not her keenest sense, it is a good idea to actively develop the visual acuity she will need for the field early. When you train your Golden to *mark/look*, you want her to actually look upward, where game will be flying. To do this, toss her toy, training dummy, or ball up in the air, and as her eyes follow it, tell her *"Sadie, look,"* then mark and reward her as her eyes track the object. Have her *mark/look* at anything in the air—planes, birds, helicopters, and so on—just to get her used to watching the skies.

Along with training her to *mark/look*, you also need to get her used to the rapid movement of you going into your gun stance. Any time you use the mark/look command, simulate the quick movement you make as you bring your gun up for the shot. You may feel foolish doing this in your backyard or out on a walk, but it is important for her to get used to this rapid movement, so she isn't startled or distracted when you finally get into the field.

Stalking

When you see your Golden begin to creep up on something (other than your neighbor's Yorkie), capture that behavior. Start with your low and slow *"Eeaasssyy,"* and then, after she has crept along slowly for a bit, give her the release *"Go get 'em!"* or *"Hunt 'em up!"*

Settle/Steady

The purpose of the command *settle* (or *steady*, whichever you prefer) is to move your Golden Retriever from excitement to a calmer physical and psychological state. The ability to curb her natural exuberance on command is valuable, whether your Golden is in your home, in the field hunting, at a competition, or working as a therapy dog.

Resting Settle

To begin, sit on the floor with your puppy between your legs. Have your puppy

lie down with her head toward your body and gently roll her over onto her back. She will probably resist at first, so in your low, slow voice tell her *"Sadie, settle."* As with the *gentle* command, think of the purr of a kitten rather than the bark of a dog. Soothingly rub her chest and continue to sweet talk her in your low, slow voice. You will begin to see signs of her relaxing as her paws go limp and flop forward; her back legs splay, opening up her lower belly area and hips; and, finally, her tail, which was most likely curled up onto her belly, relaxes and lies flat on the floor. You will also feel

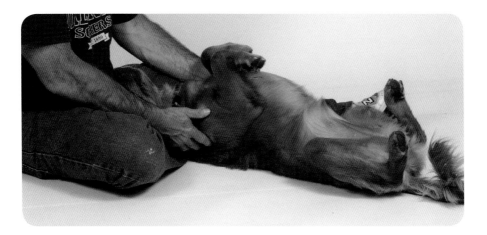

Breed Truths

The Golden Retriever's Intelligence Is Golden in the Field!

Goldens are unique in that you can teach them something, but *they* figure out the best way to do it. While some dog breeds simply repeat what they have been taught over and over, the Golden takes what she has learned and makes improvements. In other words, the Golden has the unique capacity to problem solve. This innate ability is frequently seen in the field, particularly when quartering, or moving from right to left in a pattern. If she is working a field with another dog, the Golden is intelligent enough not to rework ground that has already been covered by her partner dog. This is important because it allows you to cover more ground in a day, and hopefully locate more game.

a gradual decrease in her heart rate and respiration. At each milestone, mark and reward the behavior. Personally, I prefer the marking and reward for this exercise to be entirely verbal (quiet, low, and slow), because treats and clicks can add excitement and interrupt her calm state.

Sitting Settle

The *sitting settle* has a wide variety of applications, from keeping your Golden quiet and relaxed in a duck blind, calming her to begin a competitive event or a show, preparing her for a therapy session, or simply getting her to settle down before greeting guests in your home. While some may argue a simple *sit* will accomplish the same thing, I disagree. A simple *sit* assumes the same physical position, but it does not go far enough to move your Golden from excitement to a calmer physical and psychological state. You want her relaxed and calm. Once you and your Golden have mastered the *resting settle*, the transition to the *sitting settle* is very easy because she already understands the desired state. Simply sit your Golden in front of you, facing away from you, and lightly press on her shoulders, telling her "*Sadie, settle.*" Because she will not be able to let her body flop and relax while in a sitting position, you need to be aware of the changes in her heart rate and respiration. Again, verbally mark and reward her when you notice her calming down.

Noise Conditioning

Whether your Golden is working in the field with guns going off, as a therapy dog in noisy schools or loud medical environments, at a chaotic competitive event, or just living in a busy, active household, it is critical for her to be desensitized to a variety of sudden, loud noises. Conditioning her to loud, unexpected noises helps her to be calmer, more relaxed, and confident.

Start the noises low and soft, and gradually increase the volume. As your Golden progresses, you want a mild reaction to the noise, such as a head turn, and then a return to her activity, or, if she is sleeping, lifting her head, looking around, and then going back to sleep. If you get something more than a mild reaction, back the noise level down the next time. Try banging some pots and pans together in the next room or rolling cans on a hard floor.

Feeding your pup in the kitchen while you are doing dishes is a great way to create noise while she is focused on something else. Slamming doors and cabinets is another way to condition her to noise. If you are an inherently quiet person, you may be cringing as you read this, but trust me, it pays huge dividends as your Golden matures.

To begin desensitizing her to the sound of gunshots, softly bang two 2×4 blocks together. Begin quietly, and gradually increase the volume, keeping a close eye on her reaction so as not to spook her. Eventually you will need to introduce her to actual gunshots. However, in most urban and suburban areas, it is illegal to discharge a firearm, so you may have to opt for a cap gun or starter pistol. (Consult your local police department for the regulations governing the use of any firearm, including a starter pistol, within your community.) The challenge with a starter pistol or cap gun is that the pitch is different from an actual gunshot in the field. If you are serious about hunting your Golden Retriever, conditioning her to gunshot early is critical. Check with the local hunting club to locate a training school that offers gunshot desensitizing.

If you have a local shooting club, park a distance away from it, and every time the guns go off, say in an excited voice *"What was that?"* As she gets used to the sounds, begin to move closer.

CAUTION

Never, ever fire a gun close to a dog who has not been conditioned to the sound. The extraordinarily loud and intense noise can cause an overwhelming fear reaction in the dog, so much so that she may never be able to react calmly to gunfire. This is the perfect way to ruin a potentially great hunting dog.

Resources

Veterinary Organizations

American College of Veterinary Ophthalmologists
P.O. Box 1311
Meridian, ID 83680
Phone: (208) 466-7624
www.acvo.com

American Veterinary Medical Association
1931 North Meacham Road, Suite 100
Schaumburg, IL 60173-4360
Phone: (800) 248-2862
www.avma.org

Canine Eye Registration Foundation (CERF)
1717 Philo Road
P.O. Box 3007
Urbana, IL 61803-3007
Phone: (217) 693-4800
www.vmdb.org/cerf.html

Canine Health Information Center (CHIC)
2300 East Nifong Boulevard
Columbia, MO 65201-3806
Phone: (573) 442-0418
www.caninehealthinfo.org

Orthopedic Foundation for Animals (OFA)
2300 East Nifong Boulevard
Columbia, MO 65201-3806
Phone: (573) 442-0418
www.offa.org

University of Pennsylvania Hip Improvement Program (PennHIP)
Administrative Center
3900 Delancy Street
Philadelphia, PA 19104
Phone: (215) 573-3176
www.pennhip.org

American Holistic Veterinary Medical Association
2218 Old Emmorton Road
Bel Air, MD 21015
Phone: (410) 569-0795
www.ahvma.org

Health Studies and Articles

Hovan Slow-Grow Plan
E-mail Rhonda Hovan directly at *RhondaHovan@aol.com*

Vertical Pedigrees
http://offa.org/hovanart.pdf

Understanding Cancer in Golden Retrievers
www.vetmed.ucdavis.edu/ccah/cancer_golden%20retrievers.cfm

GRCA Health Studies
www.grca.org/health/dna-database.html
www.grca.org/health/index.html

Animal Welfare Organizations

American Society for the Prevention of Cruelty to Animals (ASPCA)
424 East 92nd Street
New York, NY 10128-6804
www.aspca.org

ASPCA Animal Poison Control Center
Phone: (888) 426-4435
(There is a consultation fee for this service.)

Humane Society of the United States
2100 L Street, NW
Washington, DC 20037
Phone: (202) 452-1100
www.hsus.org

Rescue

Golden Retriever Rescue Organizations
To locate a Golden rescue organization near you, visit the Golden Retriever Club of America's National Rescue Committee at *www.grca-nrc.org*

Breed Clubs

Golden Retriever Club of America (GRCA)
www.grca.org

GRCA Code of Ethics
www.grca.org/thegrca/code.html

Golden Retriever Club of Canada (GRCC)
www.grcc.net

Kennel Clubs

American Kennel Club (AKC)
5580 Centerview Drive
Raleigh, NC 27606-3390
Phone: (919) 233-9767
www.akc.org

The Kennel Club (United Kingdom)
1-5 Clarges Street,
Piccadilly, London W1J 8AB
Phone: 0844-463-3980
www.thekennelclub.org.uk

Kennel Club Online Services
www.the-kennel-club.org.uk/services

Canadian Kennel Club (CKC)
200 Ronson Drive, Suite 400
Etobicoke, Ontario, Canada
M9W 5Z9
Phone: (416) 675-5511
www.ckc.ca

United Kennel Club (UKC)
100 East Kilgore Road
Kalamazoo, MI 49002-5584
Phone: (269) 343-9020
www.ukcdogs.com

Animal-Assisted Therapy

The Delta Society
875 124th Avenue NE, Suite 101
Bellevue, WA 98005-2531
Phone: (425) 679-5500
www.deltasociety.org

Therapy Dogs International, Inc.
88 Bartley Road
Flanders, NJ 07836
Phone: (973) 252-9800
www.tdi-dog.org; tdi@gti.net

**R.E.A.D. (Reading Education
Assistance Program)**
Intermountain Therapy Animals
P.O. Box 17201
Salt Lake City, UT 84117
Phone: (801) 272-3439
*www.therapyanimals.org/read;
info@therapyanimals.org*

Other Organizations and Activities

The AKC, CKC, and UKC offer a variety of club-sponsored activities.

North American Flyball Association
1400 West Devon Avenue, #512
Chicago, IL 60660
Phone: (800) 318-6312
www.flyball.org

**World Canine Freestyle
Organization**
P.O. Box 350122
Brooklyn, NY 11235
Phone: (718) 332-8336
www.worldcaninefreestyle.org

**Musical Dog Sport Association
(MDSA)**
9211 West Road, #143-104
Houston, TX 77064
www.musicaldogsport.com

**National Association for
Search and Rescue, Inc.**
www.nasar.org

DockDogs
5183 Silver Maple Lane
Medina, OH 44256
Phone: (330) 241-4975
www.dockdogs.com

**North American Dog Agility
Council (NADAC)**
P.O. Box 1206
Colbert, OK 74733
www.nadac.com

**United States Dog Agility
Association (USDAA)**
P.O. Box 850955
Richardson, TX 75085
Phone: (972) 487-2200
www.usdaa.com

Periodicals

Golden Retriever News (for GRCA
members only)
www.grca.org/thegrca/grcanews.html

The American Kennel Club Gazette
51 Madison Avenue
New York, NY 10010
www.akc.org/pubs/gazette

Gun Dog Magazine
P.O. Box 420234
Palm Coast, FL 32142-0234
www.gundogmag.com

The Retriever Journal
P.O. Box 509
Traverse City, MI 49685
Phone: (800) 447-7367
www.retrieverjournal.com

The BARk
2810 8th Street
Berkeley, CA 94710
www.thebark.com

The Whole Dog Journal
P.O. Box 420234
Palm Coast, FL 32142-0234
Phone: (800) 829-9165
www.whole-dog-journal.com

Books

Adamson, Eve. *The Golden Retriever.* Neptune, NJ: T. F. H. Publications, 2005.

Alderton, David. *Young at Heart.* Pleasantville, NY: The Reader's Digest Association, Inc., 2007.

Aloff, Brenda. *Canine Body Language: A Photographic Guide.* Wenatchee, WA: Dogwise Publishing, 2005.

American Kennel Club Dog Care and Training. New York: Hungry Minds, Inc., 2002.

Benjamin, Carol Lea. *Surviving Your Dog's Adolescence.* New York: Howell Book House, 1993.

Cairns, Julie. *The Golden Retriever: All That Glitters.* New York: Wiley Publishing, Inc., 1999.

Coile, D. Caroline. *The Golden Retriever Handbook.* Hauppauge, NY: Barron's Educational Series Inc., 2000.

Coren, Stanley. *How Dogs Think.* New York: Free Press, 2004.

Eldredge, Debra M., et al. *Dog Owner's Home Veterinary Handbook.* Hoboken, NJ: Wiley Publishing, Inc., 2007.

Falk, John R. *Gun Dogs: Playful Pup to Hunting Partner.* Osceola, WI: Voyageur Press 2003

____. *The Complete Guide to Bird Dog Training.* Guilford, CT: The Lyons Press 1976.

Fennell, Jan. *The Dog Listener.* New York: HarperCollins Publishers, Inc., 2004.

____. *The Seven Ages of Man's Best Friend.* New York: HarperCollins Publishers, Inc., 2005.

Foss, Valerie (editor). *The Ultimate Golden Retriever.* New York: Howell Book House, 1997.

Heegaard, Marge Eaton. *Saying Goodbye to Your Pet.* Minneapolis, MN: Fairview Press, 2001.

Lamb, Vickie. *The Ultimate Hunting Reference Book.* Guilford, CT: The Lyons Press, 2007.

McConnell, Patricia. *For the Love of a Dog.* New York: Ballantine Books, 2005.

____. *Tales of Two Species.* Wenatchee, WA: Dogwise Publishing, 2009.

____. *The Other End of the Leash.* New York: Ballantine Books, 2002.

Morgan, Diane. *The Living Well Guide for Senior Dogs.* Neptune, NJ: T. F. H. Publications, 2007.

Nicholas, Anna Katherine. *The Book of the Golden Retriever.* Neptune, NJ: T. F. H. Publications, 1983.

Yin, Sophia. *How to Behave So Your Dog Behaves.* Neptune, NJ: T. F. H. Publications, 2004.